*Donated
In Memory of*

Louis A. King

and

Marion B. King

Firehouse

This Large Print Book carries the
Seal of Approval of N.A.V.H.

Firehouse

David Halberstam

WHEELER
PUBLISHING

The times used throughout for the impact of the planes and the collapse of the towers have been verified with information from the Seismology Group at the Lamont-Doherty Earth Observatory at Columbia University.

Published in 2002 by arrangement with
Hyperion, an imprint of Buena Vista Books, Inc.

Wheeler Hardcover Series.

The text of this Large Print edition is unabridged.
Other aspects of the book may vary from the original edition.

Front jacket photographs © Will Ryan.

Set in 16 pt. Plantin by Al Chase.

Printed in the United States on permanent paper.

Library of Congress Control Number: 2002106172

ISBN 1-58724-260-5 (lg. print : hc : alk. paper)

Firehouse

ONE

The Upper West Side of Manhattan, just above Columbus Circle, was until quite recently a relatively poor neighborhood, and some of the veteran firemen at Engine 40, Ladder 35, located at Sixty-sixth Street and Amsterdam Avenue, like to recall how Amsterdam was once the dividing line between an Irish neighborhood to the east and a black neighborhood, just to the west. The black neighborhood used to be known as San Juan Hill, some say in honor of the black soldiers who moved there after the Spanish-American War, or perhaps because of the frequent, bloody street fights that occurred between the Irish and black kids early in the century, or finally because some of the city's earliest Puerto Rican settlers lived there. But after World War II, as the city became ever more affluent, as every piece of real estate in Manhattan became more and more valuable, the neighborhood began to change. The tenements that had housed the poor, where bookies haunted the hallways and homing pigeons were sometimes still kept on the roofs, and the cheap single-room occupancy (SRO) hotels, in which rooms rented for five dollars a night, began to disappear, to be replaced by solidly middle-class apartment buildings. The process accelerated in 1959 with the groundbreaking for Lincoln Center, a vast new cultural complex that would house the Metropolitan Opera, the New York City Ballet, the New York Philharmonic, and the Juilliard School.

In the early 1960s skyscrapers began to sprout into the sky like giant steel-and-glass fingers. What had before been barely a blue-collar neighborhood became not merely middle class, but in time, upper-middle class. The firemen and cops who worked the area, many of whose families lived in the neighborhood and in other working-class sections of Manhattan, were caught in this relentless process of economic and social change, and they began to move, first to the boroughs — Queens, Brooklyn, and Staten Island — and then, in the last twenty years, to the satellite commuter communities surrounding New York City, on Long Island, and north of the city in Rockland County, New York, and in New Jersey.

The firehouse of Engine 40, Ladder 35, that stands guard over this ever more affluent neighborhood was originally built in 1961. It was a pleasant if not very fancy building, spacious with enough of a yard in back for the men to play basketball and for them to sit outside and barbecue food on hot summer nights. But in the 1980s the air rights above the firehouse were sold, and a sixty-story apartment house of the very kind that

8

is a nightmare for any New York fireman was erected, ironically enough, right on top of the firehouse. The men were forced out during the construction of the towering building, and from 1988 to 1994 they were housed in the tunnels under Lincoln Center on Amsterdam, at Sixty-third Street. It was not the most pleasant of temporary bases, being windowless and dank, and there were in time numerous jokes about the fact that any children conceived by the men during this period might end up looking like moles. The men began to refer to themselves as the Cavemen, which eventually became the company's nickname, and since, much like military units, firehouses often have patches designating their units, the patch for 40/35 featured two Cavemen — a couple of firefighters looking as if they had recently escaped from a *Flintstones* cartoon.

The renovated station house, when it was finally completed, turned out to be quite ordinary, gray and functional, easy to pass by without gaining a second look. It gave off none of the wonderful aura of a classic firehouse. When the men moved back, they also discovered that it had been reconfigured, regrettably, to significantly smaller specifications. Everything felt tighter and more constricted. The backyard that had given them such pleasure was gone. The kitchen, so important in any firehouse as the center of social life, was now unacceptably small; there was one good-sized room where the

9

men were to eat, but it was hemmed in by two much smaller rooms, one in which food was to be stored and prepared and the dishes washed, the other simply a storage room. The architect, the men grumbled, had not known a damn thing about being a fireman or how firemen lived. Over time there was considerable talk about breaking down the walls and making all three rooms into one larger one. But doing that — changing the architect's plans — would have meant fighting through an immense amount of red tape, at the very least.

Although there were many opinions about what to do, there was almost no opposition to the idea of one larger room. So one weekend Bruce Gary, a chauffeur on the engine (that is a driver of Engine 40, a crucial role in the firehouse), a man who by dint of his awesome physical strength and equally formidable personal integrity was an imposing figure within the station's political and social order, decided that the debate about whether or not to expand had gone on for long enough. Even though they were supposed to consult with the department on matters such as building alterations, the time had come to act unilaterally, he believed. So Gary simply took a sledgehammer and started knocking down the offending walls.

That day Jim Gormley, who at the time was a lieutenant in the house, wandered into the building and was told by another lieutenant, Pete Gorman, just to go to his office because he did not want to know what was going on — which, of course, he did not. As Bruce Gary was finishing his demolition, he was approached by one of his younger colleagues who informed him that he could not do what he was doing. "Can't do it?" Gary repeated in disbelief. "What the hell do you mean I can't do it — I just did it." That ended the debate; not many people wanted to challenge Bruce Gary — on something like this anyway.

Firemen live in a world apart from other civilians. The rest of the world seems to change, but the firehouses do not. This is, in fact, as close to a hermetically sealed world as you are likely to find in contemporary America: It is driven by its unique needs, norms, and traditions, some of which are inviolable. The New York Fire Department is largely male — women have in recent years become firefighters, but that has happened slowly, and many houses have remained all-male, including 40/35 — and largely white, and it is to an uncommon degree composed of men who come from firefighting families, men who, like their fathers before them, have wanted to be firemen since childhood.

A great deal of the tradition and the coherence is family-driven, with generation after generation supplying men to the department. It is almost as if there is a certain DNA strand found in firefighting families, where the men are pulled toward the job because their fathers and uncles were firemen and had loved it, and because some of their happiest moments when they were boys had come when they visited the firehouse and these big, gruff men made a fuss over them. The job and the mission and the sense of purpose that go with it have always been quietly blended into the family fabric. "It's passed on father to son, and sometimes grandfather to father to son," says the Reverend Robert Scholz, who is the pastor of a Lutheran church located about three blocks from the 40/35 firehouse and who knows the men well. "You see your father doing it, and you're proud of him. His life seems honorable and purposeful, and you see the richness of his friendships and the loyalty of these men to each other, and how, when you're young, the other firemen seem like additional uncles. And it seems so honorable."

All of this makes the department's hold on the men quite striking in an age when the lure of material and other ego rewards is so powerful. The hold the New York Fire Department has on the young men of the city and its environs is as strong as ever. The waiting list to get into the department is long, so long that many young men who want to be firemen start as cops and transfer to the fire department when their numbers finally come up. Yet the pay is marginal. According to one department veteran, a young married fireman with four children and a wife who doesn't work makes so little that he is technically eligible for food stamps. Almost all of the men at 40/35 could double their pay in other jobs.

Terry Holden, who has been at 40/35 since 1964 and who has seen the personnel turn over more than once, says of the unusual sense of continuity: "It's completely different from when I first came here. There's not a single person left from back then. And the country and the city are very different, and yet the house in most important ways is exactly the same — even though it's a completely different generation from a very different era. It's as if we've been cloned. Part of it is that the talent pool is so similar — we come from the same places, the same kind of families, sometimes even the same parochial schools, and we have the same values. And we still have the same purpose, though we don't like to talk about it openly. But we like it when we get back to the firehouse after a fire and someone says you did a good job. Especially when you tell that to the junior men."

A firehouse, most firemen believe, is like a vast extended second family — rich, warm, joyous, and supportive, but on occasion quite edgy as well, with all the inevitable tensions brought on by so many forceful men living so closely together over so long a period of time. What gradually emerges is surprisingly nuanced; the cumulative human texture has slowly evolved over time and is often delicate. It is created out of hundreds of unseen, unknown, and often unidentified tiny adjustments that these strong, willful men make to accommodate one another, sometimes agreeably and sometimes grudgingly. It incorporates how the men live with one another day in and day out, and surprisingly the degree to which, whether they realize it or not, they come to love one another (sometimes even as they dislike one another) — because love is a critical ingredient in the fireman's code, which demands that you are willing to risk your life for your firehouse brothers.

The men not only live and eat with one another, they play sports together, go off to drink together, help repair one another's houses, and, most important, share terrifying risks; their loyalties to one another, by the demands of the dangers they face, must be instinctive and absolute. Thus are firehouse codes fashioned. When a probie — a probationary or apprentice firefighter — joins a firehouse, he must adjust to the firehouse culture, rather than the firehouse adjusting to him. It is like the military in that respect: Idiosyncrasy can come later; adherence to the rules and traditions comes first.

Reverend Scholz long ago decided that there was something special to firemen and their traditions, that they had chosen this profession because it expanded their lives and gave those lives additional meaning. Many of the men, he said, were not necessarily angels or saintly — far from it, in fact — and they were not, in the traditional sense, necessarily very religious. But there was also a certain spiritual redemption to what they

14

did. They could be on occasion rowdy and combative and they had their allotted share of human flaws, of which they themselves were often all too aware. But whatever they had done wrong the night before, the next morning when they were at the firehouse, they were able to take extra meaning from their lives, and to find some form of redemption because of the nature of the job, because of the risks they take for complete strangers.

Scholz believed that outsiders would never be able to understand who these men were and what they did unless they understood the job for what it is — nothing less than a calling. Jim Gormley, now captain of Engine 40, completely agreed. "We all have our daily conversation with God," Gormley once said. "Do we do what we do for God? No. But it's there, the religious part, just the same. We do it for people. We do it for the sense of rightness. And we like doing it, like the life because we're never ashamed of what we do."

The men are loath to talk about the daily risks, even with their wives. "People think they know what we do, but they don't really know what we do," says 40/35 veteran Ray Pfeifer of the real danger, of being in a burning building when there is a collapse and the exits seem blocked. It is not unusual for a firehouse to lose a man to a fire periodically. And there are those awful times, graven in everyone's minds, when there is a truly devastating fire, when the Fates are more powerful than all the skills and resources of the firefighters. This happened in Astoria, Queens, on Father's Day 2001, when a fire broke out in a hardware store, cans of paint and chemicals exploded, and three men died.

All firemen in all firehouses tend to think that theirs is the best of all firehouses, a chosen place, one with the highest sense of duty, with the toughest mission, and the greatest sense of élan, but it is true that the men of 40/35, located as they are in midtown Manhattan, feel this even more passionately than most. It is considered an unusually strong house, filled with veterans who do not want to transfer out. Content to remain firemen, they often do not want to take the exam to become officers. This is not just because they like being firemen and like passing on their unique traditions to the younger men, but also because they love this particular house; if they became officers, they would have to go elsewhere. As such, 40/35 has an unusually high sense of cohesion and loyalty. When a young fireman named Kevin Shea did so well during his three years of rotating among firehouses that he was allowed to choose his house, he did a good deal of checking around and was told by a number of senior people to try 40/35. "It's the hidden jewel in Manhattan," Captain Gary Ruiz, a battalion chief told him, recalling that his seven years there, before he had been promoted, were among his happiest as a fireman.

About fifty men work at 40/35 in shifts, eleven

at any given time. Eight of the men are officers — two captains and six lieutenants. The house contains both engine and ladder (or truck — when the firehouse terminology is written out, it is Engine 40 and Ladder 35; when it is spoken among the firemen, it is always 40 Engine and 35 Truck). By tradition and assigned role, it is the truck that finds the fire in a given building, and whose men search for any survivors and get them out of the building; the men on the engine pump the water, attack the fire, and finally put it out. The rivalry between truck and engine and the competition over whose role is more important and who are the *real* firemen are constant, and given the raucous nature of firehouse humor (if firefighting was easy, goes the joke, the cops would do it), sharply edged. The engine men like to refer to the truckees as firemen's helpers. Once a year the firehouse has Medal Day, and, the engine men say, most of the medals are inevitably bestowed upon truckees because they are the ones who do most of the rescuing. "Privately we call it Truck Appreciation Day," says Pfeifer, a 40 Engine guy. "We feel they really deserve the medals because we're so busy putting out the fires and having all the real fun, so they ought to get something to compensate."

The truckees say that all engine men are terrible cooks, that the engines get lost all the time, and cannot find a fire without the help of the truck. Because of that, they can never go anywhere alone. Besides, the truckees note, since

17

the engine men have to get down low to fight a fire, sometimes crawling once they're inside a building to get under the heat, all engine men are short and stubby. To which counters Pfeifer, firemen are selected for their different roles — engine or truck — when they're still at the academy. "The doctor comes in with a stethoscope and he checks out the young fireman's heartbeat, and if it's strong, a real *thump-thump-thump*, then you go to the engine. But if it's fainter, something of a *pitter-patter*, then it's to the truck."

No one did the engine-truck humor more caustically than Bruce Gary. Truckees were, in his vernacular, Big Dumb Truckees, or BDTs. Once last year Ladder 35 had had to cover for Ladder 15, down on South Street, which was out on a run. It was not a trip the men had wanted to make, and nothing had gone well. The call had come late in the day, all of their plans for the evening were obviously shot. It had been a bad enough day anyway, but, as they were leaving, they heard Bruce Gary's voice as he sang over the firehouse's loudspeaker system his own version of the old song "South Street": "Where do all the dummies go? . . . On South Street, on South Street . . ."

One of the things that the men particularly like about 40/35 is that they have to deal with a variety of fires — fires in tenements (a few remain), fires in brownstones (generally considered easier), and, of course, fires in high-rises. There

18

are not as many fires as the men working in ghetto neighborhoods have to contend with — sometimes during what are now known as the "war years" of the late '60s, '70s, and even '80s, the ghetto firemen were called out on as many as three or four real jobs a day — but skyscraper fires are infinitely more dangerous and harder to control because the buildings are so much bigger.

Everything is more complex and more dangerous in mid-Manhattan. Firemen who work in the outer boroughs like to think that Manhattan firemen have it easy, that it is a plush assignment, and occasionally someone from one of the boroughs who has never struggled with a highrise fire will talk about Manhattan's being a firemen's retirement community, because there is less action. But the men at 40/35 talk as readily about the men from the boroughs who rotate in to fill a slot and who, sampling their first highrise fire, are ready to leave the next day — they want no part of it. Mid-Manhattan, says Jim Gormley, "is a carnivore. It doesn't eat often, but when it does, it eats hungrily."

Gormley is the son of a fireman — his father, Hubert Gormley, had been a Deputy Borough Commissioner in New York — and his sense of the dangers of Manhattan, where buildings seem to be ever higher, is acute. The worst fire Jim Gormley ever caught at 40/35 was in January 1997. It was known in the neighborhood as the Lionel Hampton Fire, because it started at the famed vibraphone player's apartment, at Sixty-fourth Street and Columbus Avenue, only three blocks from the firehouse. The Hampton fire had all the right ingredients to end in real tragedy: Hampton lived on the twenty-eighth floor of a forty-three-story building, it was a violently windy day, the windows in the apartment had either popped or been broken because the heat was so great, the door to the apartment had been left open, and the materials in the apartment were highly flammable. In short, the apartment turned into nothing less than a giant flue, Gormley, then still a lieutenant, recalled. The Ninth Battalion chief, Joe Grosso, known among the men as "The High-Rise Drifter" because he looked like Clint Eastwood, took one look at the fire and asked for all the help he could get. Over 200 firefighters from more than fifty units responded. The heat was so intense that the firemen could not last long fighting it — it made them go through their air tanks too fast. Because of that, men had to be rotated in and out as quickly as possible. When Gormley first arrived, he saw Hampton, who was confined to a wheelchair, and his nurse in the lobby. Gormley got the keys to the apartment from the nurse and asked her if she had closed the door (thus limiting the spread of the fire), and she said yes; but when he got up to the twenty-eighth floor, it turned out she was wrong — the door was open, allowing the fire to draw with a ferocity all its own.

Gormley had never seen or heard anything like it before. He felt the terrible heat when he was still behind a closed door one floor below. The noise of the fire was a giant, terrifying roar, like a gargantuan engine churning at fever pitch. Down on the street, there were connections for two hoses, and they poured more than 500 gallons of water a minute into the fire, but the fire was so hot that the water turned into steam just a few feet from the nozzle. It took firefighters twenty-four minutes to battle the fifty-four feet from the staircase to the fire, even with the two water lines. It was the first time in his long career that Gormley thought, *This is it, this is the one that I might not make it back from.* He and his men did their first tour, went downstairs and got fresh air tanks, then did a second. Two young women were working in an office on the same floor as the Hampton apartment, and somehow Stan Sussina, a fireman from Rescue One, an elite Special Operations Command unit, managed to save them. Sussina was lowered down by rope from the twenty-ninth floor, crashed through the window, placed breathing masks on the women, and got them out. Miraculously, though twenty-seven people were injured, no one was killed at the Lionel Hampton Fire. For months after, however, when Jim Gormley thought about the fire, he could still feel the heat on his face, legs, and back.

TWO

The schedules for that fateful morning, September 11, 2001, are still on the two house blackboards, unchanged, exactly as they were written out. They stand as if time had stopped on that terrible day — which in some ways it has for Engine Company 40, Ladder Company 35. On top of one blackboard someone had written "CARRY A CHOCK!!" Then the blackboards give the slots and the names:

ENGINE 40		**LADDER 35**	
DATE	9/11/01	DATE	9/11/01
TOUR	6 x 9	TOUR	9 x 6
OFFICER	Lt Ginley	OFFICER	Capt. Callahan
E.C.C.	Gary	CHAUF.	Giberson
NOZZLE	Lynch, M.	O.V.M.	Otten
BACK UP	D'Auria	ROOF	Roberts

ENGINE 40   LADDER 35

DOOR	Marshall E-23	IRONS	Morrello
STAND PIPE	Mercado	CAN	Bracken E40
			Shea

If any one moment brought home the sheer human horror of that day, it was when John Morello, father of Vincent Morello, one of the men from 40/35, found out what had happened. In the early-morning hours of Wednesday, September 12, John, a retired battalion chief, was still trying to determine what had happened to Vincent, who was listed as being on Ladder 35 and was missing. Communications with fire authorities had been terrible; the city's Emergency Command Center in 7 World Trade Center had been destroyed early in the terrorist attack, and any real information had been sketchy.

It had been some seventeen hours since the Ladder 35 rig left the house, and Morello, fearful of the worst, but having no inkling how bad the worst really was, had been calling various private department phone numbers he knew. He was by this time with his daughter-in-law Debi at her and Vincent's home in Middle Village, Queens. Finally, around 2:30 a.m., he got through to someone. Morello explained that he was a retired battalion chief and that his son had been down at the World Trade Center. The man at the other end of the line agreed to help him. Morello did not realize that Debi was listening in on the first-floor extension. "Thirty-five Truck," the man had said. "Thirty-five Truck is missing."

"What the hell does that mean, Thirty-five Truck is missing?" Morello asked. "The whole company is missing?"

"Yes," said the man at the other end, "the whole company is missing." That was when John Morello heard Debi on the line, screaming in agony, not just for herself, it seemed, but for every family member connected to 40/35 and all the other New York firehouses that day.

September 11 was a special kind of hell for 40/35. No one who works at the firehouse has really yet comprehended the apocalyptic nature of what occurred. That morning thirteen men set out on the house's two rigs, and twelve of them died. It was a tragedy beyond comprehension, not just the worst day in the history of New York City, but one of the worst days in American history — a day that people would compare to Pearl Harbor, sixty years earlier. The New York Fire Department was the institution that bore the brunt of it — 343 men killed — and the 40/35 firehouse was among the hardest hit. The aftershocks of the tragedy have persisted not just in the grief for the men who were lost, but also in the guilt among the survivors, who have continued to wonder not just why they lived, but whether it was wrong to have done so. There have been acceptable days, and there have been bad days, when the pain was almost unbearable.

The men of 40/35 are bonded now more than ever, not just by their job, as in the past, but by their grief as well. Sometimes the house has the feeling of a World War II unit, in which a good part of the men were wiped out in one sudden, shocking battle, and none of the survivors entirely understands what happened — why so many men were taken so cruelly and so quickly, and why they, the survivors, were spared. So much of who went that morning and who did not was chance. Some were relieved early and were on their way home before they heard about the attack; some were supposed to have worked that day but had taken what are called mutuals, which meant that, for personal reasons, they had switched shifts with other men.

Bob Menig, a thirty-seven-year-old Ladder 35 veteran, had been scheduled to go out to Long Island for an often delayed doctor's appointment, one that he had been told not to miss. It was set for 9:00 a.m. Tuesday in Valley Stream. That meant that Menig, whose shift was over at nine, had to leave half an hour early, so he asked his relief, Mike D'Auria, a popular young probie who had not yet graduated from the academy, to come in a bit early. In order to do so D'Auria spent Monday night at the firehouse, rather than going home to Staten Island. Even so, at 8:30, when Menig had to leave for the appointment, the house was still one fireman short, because

25

Dan Marshall, who was being sent over from a neighboring firehouse at the last minute to fill a vacancy, had not yet arrived. Marshall was supposed to relieve Vincent Morello, and in this kind of situation at least one fireman must stay and cover, drawing overtime for so-called waiting relief. Morello asked Menig if he wanted to wait relief, and Menig said that normally he would, but on this day he had to get to his doctor's appointment. "Is that okay?" Menig had asked Morello. "No sweat," Morello had answered. With that, Menig left for his appointment.

As he was driving on the Long Island Expressway, Menig heard a sketchy, preliminary report on the radio about a plane hitting one of the Twin Towers. He immediately called the firehouse on his car phone, and Morello answered. "Vinnie, is it a big plane or a little plane?" Menig asked, and Morello answered that it was a big plane, and that they had already gotten the fifth alarm. "I can't wait to get down there," Morello said and then told Menig not to worry.

Afterward, Bob Menig was one of the men who took the tragedy hardest. He had been spared by such a fluky chain of events, he thought, and his dealings with two of the men who died later that morning made it all the worse, the guilt all the more immediate. In his mind he replayed what had happened over and over — *he* was the person who had asked

26

D'Auria to come in early to fill in for him, *he* was the person who had not been able to wait relief for Vinnie Morello. Menig was unsparing in his self-examination, and it tormented him every day. He worried that because of his choices — even if they were not choices, for his doctor's appointment was essentially mandatory — he might have had a hand in causing the deaths of two men. It was almost more than he could bear. Menig tried therapy but did not find it especially helpful. What did help, and gave him as much solace as he was able to accept, was talking to the other men at the firehouse, who were going through similar anguish, and to Marc Morello, Vinnie's older brother, also a fireman, who had come over to 40/35 on temporary duty after the tragedy.

It was as if there were an enormous hole in the house. As Matt Malecki, one of the veteran 40/35 firemen, said, what was hard was the constancy of the loss, the fact that it would never go away. Sometimes for a brief moment, he noted, you would catch yourself thinking, well, they're just off on vacation and they'll be back. But then, almost immediately, the truth would return, and you would realize that they were never coming back, and you would have to accept the hard reality of that. It meant that a new social fabric had to be created within the house, not the same one as before, but similar, with new men, like it or not, taking on the roles left behind by such veterans as Bruce Gary and Jimmy Giberson, who

27

did so much to set the tone for the company.

The station house, like so many others in New York City, became, in the days after, something of a shrine. The names and photos of the men who died were posted near the door. People, strangers mostly, still come by to leave flowers, notes, and cards there. To no small degree it has the same feel as the Vietnam Memorial in Washington, in the sense of it being a homemade memorial. In the first few days after the tragedy, a young woman in her twenties would stop every morning, look at the pictures, and then burst into tears. Finally one of the firemen asked her what was the matter, had she lost a close friend in the firehouse? No, she answered, but she felt as if she knew one of the firemen, and then she pointed to the photo of Giberson, a big, strapping, good-looking man, who had been a chauffeur on Ladder 35. In the photo he was wearing a hat because he *always* wore a hat. Giberson, who was forty-three at the time of his death, had been quite sensitive about losing his hair, and one of his idiosyncrasies was what the men called "the hat switch." It was not something they teased him about — he was too strong and forceful to be teased about something like that — but everyone knew that Giberson always wore a baseball cap around the firehouse, and his fireman's hat on the truck, and when it was time to go out on a run, Giberson would switch the baseball cap with the fireman's hat as fast as possible, when he thought no one was looking.

Jimmy Giberson always started slowly in the morning, and the other men knew it and did not crowd him then. One of his small pleasures was to come in a little early, when the city around him was just beginning to stir and the people in the neighborhood were going off to work. He would take his coffee in front of the firehouse and watch everyone hurrying by. He would smile and say hello, as if the better to understand the people in the neighborhood whose lives he was charged with protecting. That was when the young woman had seen him, and though they had never said more than hello to each other, and she did not even know his name, she had come to think of him as her personal fireman.

That morning had started lazily enough. There had been little action during the previous three days. Labor Day had come and gone and now the summer was unofficially finished, vacations were used up, children were going back to school. Over the weekend the big event had been an alarm from a box a block from the firehouse, which turned out to have been caused by some kind of mechanical error in the box. The weather was brilliant, and the city seemed unusually empty and quiet, with many people still away at their summer homes, trying to squeeze out a little more vacation. A primary election was being held, in which New Yorkers were to choose the candidates for a new mayor, among other officials, but it had stirred little excitement, and the turnout was expected to be very low.

Among the 40/35 men were a number of golfers — how good they were was a subject of constant debate at the firehouse kitchen table. Several of them — Greg Petrik, Mike Kotula, Anthony Rucco, Ray Pfeifer, and Joe Mackey — were still away on a golfing weekend in Ocean City, Maryland. Two other firemen, Michael Boyle and David Arce (Arce was known generally by his nickname, Buddha), who worked out of Engine 33 on Great Jones Street in Manhattan, had originally been scheduled to go along on the trip. The two had both recently rotated through 40/35, and they remained de facto members of the house and still played on the 40/35 softball team. But at the last minute Boyle decided not to go, because he was active in politics and wanted to spend the primary day campaigning in Queens for his cousin Matt Farrell, who was running for city council. Arce had offered to help him out. Rucco was quite disappointed Boyle and Buddha were not coming; the way he saw it, politics was getting in the way of really important things, like golf.

Most people thought Arce was called Buddha because he was so quiet, but in truth he had gotten the nickname in childhood, when he played cards and carried around a Buddha bank in which to stow his poker winnings. On every deal of the cards, Arce would rub the belly of the Buddha bank for luck. He had grown up a few doors away from Boyle in Westbury, Long Island, and had been virtually drafted into the Boyle clan and thus into the world of firemen, since the Boyles were a legendary firefighting family. The paterfamilias, Jimmy Boyle, had served as a much-loved head of the firefighters' union.

Buddha and Boyle remained inseparable best friends in adulthood, and Buddha followed Boyle by a year on rotations through three houses — Engine 33, then Ladder 35, and then Engine 226. As Boyle departed each house, he would tell the men there to take care of his buddy, and Buddha took care of Boyle too. After Boyle had gotten a bit too boisterous once at a firehouse golf outing, it was Buddha who had lobbied for nearly a year to get him permission to go on the next one. In the eyes of most of the men at 40/35, Buddha was nothing less than a brilliant fireman, and Mike Boyle was also someone special, the scion of an important firefighting family, active in department politics, a young man who might one day himself head the Uniformed Firefighters Association. Plus, Boyle was engaged to marry Rosemary Kenny, the daughter of fireman Mark Kenny, who had recently retired from Engine 40.

That Saturday both Boyle and Buddha had participated in the Marty Celic Running Festival, a four-mile race on Staten Island honoring a firefighter who had died battling an arson fire in lower Manhattan in 1977. They were representing their own firehouse, Engine 33, which had been looking for its fourth Celic victory in a row. Boyle was a good marathon runner and was hoping to break three hours in the upcoming New York Marathon in November, while Buddha was better at shorter distances. While they were at the race, Anthony Rucco was shopping for golf clothes for the Maryland trip. Suddenly his cell phone beeped. It was Boyle on the other end of the line, screaming so loudly that at first Rucco had trouble understanding him. *"Anthony! Four-peat! Four-peat! We did it again!"* Boyle was yelling. Rucco finally figured out that Boyle was trying to tell him they had won again. Both men had run very well that day, and Boyle was beside himself with excitement — later Buddha had had trouble getting him to leave the race because Boyle was so busy talking to and celebrating with everyone there. Rucco had been pleased for his friends, but he was a little sad that they weren't coming on the golfing trip — they were both on such a high that it would have been great fun to have them along.

At 8:00 a.m. that Tuesday morning the house was bustling. That was one of the best times of the day, the firemen thought, because it was an hour before the change of shifts, and most of the men tended to come in early, and so the house was full of people, exchanging gossip, some of it pure firehouse talk, some of it more social in origin. With the weather outside so strikingly clear and the temperature around seventy degrees, everyone was relaxed. That two planes had already taken off from Boston's Logan Airport and were to be hijacked and aimed like missiles at the World Trade Center was something no one at 40/35 could yet know.

Captain Frank Callahan, the senior officer in the house that morning, had been a fireman for just under twenty-eight years and a captain at 40/35 for three. He was an old-fashioned man, the other firemen thought, very much a throwback to another era when the officers did not lightly mix with the men. There was a certain emotional distance to him, and he did not encourage intimacy or pal-ship. He did not readily tell them that they had done a good job, and that too was a throwback to another age in America, one when life was harder and more austere, when compliments and kind words were more carefully rationed. In those years fathers did not lightly praise their children, and bosses did not easily praise their employees, in no small part because no one had praised them when they were growing up. It was a culture in which the absence of criticism was regarded as praise enough, and doing the job for the job's sake was viewed as reward enough.

Most people understood the need for some degree of distance between the officers and the men; Callahan's friend Captain John Dunne, who had worked with him in Brooklyn at Ladder 105, thought such distance was a necessary part

33

of the job, "because when you're the captain, it's like being the father of twenty-five terrific but incorrigible kids. You need the distance." But there was no doubt that Frank Callahan preferred a little more distance than most other officers.

On the first day when Callahan had shown up to take command of 35 Truck, in July 1998, no one in the house knew very much about him. Several of the men had hung around expressly to greet and welcome him. They intended, of course, to size him up as well. Callahan arrived, carrying his own gear. When he saw the men, he put it down and gave them a cool appraising look, neither friendly nor unfriendly; it was not the cold, hard stare that they would come to know all too well later on, when they had performed poorly at a fire, but rather a neutral glance, which on the first day implied, one of the men thought, that they were not to feel too good about themselves. Then without saying a single word — not even his name in introduction — Callahan turned and went upstairs to his office. That, naturally enough, had made the men nervous. It was a very clear signal that he was already measuring them.

In the world of big-city firemen an enormous amount of information is constantly being passed through back channels; everyone, it seems, has worked with someone else at some other firehouse during rotations, or has a brother or a cousin or a father who has worked with a particular fireman, and so there is always someone who has the book on anyone new coming in. The men checked around, and someone knew Charlie Bonar, who had worked with Callahan when they were young firemen, and the word eventually came back: Frank Callahan was a bit distant, very quiet — they would not get a lot of words out of him — but he was a very good fireman. He was, Bonar and others warned, likely to be quite exacting with them; they would do well to be at their very best, and not to take anything with him for granted.

Callahan, it turned out, was nothing if not exacting; if the men did something wrong at a fire, he would go over it with them immediately, and not necessarily gently. Clearly, in his eyes there was a right way and a wrong way to do everything. In time, though they thought a little more warmth might have been helpful, and a touch of the avuncular a bit welcome, the men came to respect how dedicated and professional Callahan was. They realized that what he wanted was their very best, and that he did not shirk from such excellence himself; he did not talk one game and then play another. So if he was somewhat severe and aloof, they could live with that. The men will, as Captain Jim Gormley once noted, work very hard to protect a good officer and to keep him in place, because by protecting him, they are protecting themselves. Therefore they performed at a very high level for Callahan, and the reason was simple enough —

35

they did not want him to be replaced by a lesser man.

In those early months, though, the scrutiny of him was intense as they tried to figure out what made him work. The captain's character is elemental to the code of the firehouse, for he holds in his hands the men's very survival, regularly making decisions of life and death. By tradition the captain is the first in and the last out of any fire. It is one of the things, firefighters think, that differentiates them from the police. The higher you rise among the cops, firemen believe, the less likely you are to expose yourself to harm; police officials tend to arrive on the scene after the heat of battle. But that is not true of firemen. When you become an officer in a firehouse, your burden and need to expose yourself to danger only increase. The officers lead the men into the fire and share their dangers. Thus leadership and title are not merely hierarchical with firemen, they are the basis of a sacred trust, and so officers are viewed through a brutal prism. But that did not turn out to be a problem for Frank Callahan. Week by week, month by month, he won their trust.

Not everyone did. A few years earlier there had been an officer who had come into the house determined to make his mark by letting the men know who was in charge. He was a strutter; one of those officers, the men said, who swaggered when he was sitting down. He operated from the start as a hard nose, always showing everyone how tough he was and how they had better shape up in order to meet his high standards. That was bad enough in a veteran house such as 40/35. What was worse was that they did not like what they saw of him as a fireman. The fascinating thing about a firehouse as a workplace, thought Terry Holden, is the unspoken truth: *Everyone knows everything about everyone, and therefore nothing can be faked.* Because of the nature of the profession, because of the risks taken daily, nothing can be hidden. The men are always watching and measuring one another, and, above all, watching and measuring their officers. They do it because they have to. That kind of scrutiny is nothing less than mandatory; words in a firehouse matter much less than deeds — it is a place where no one dares use the modern art of spin, so valued in most other places in America. It is not a place for the slick or the facile. The result is that everyone inevitably comes to know all too well everyone else's strengths and flaws. And so the men of 40/35 had almost immediately discovered that not only did this new officer swagger and push them hard on superficial things, but he was, when it really mattered — at a fire — not very aggressive. He lacked the elemental, fearless instinct that a good officer needs.

Some of the senior men quietly tried to talk to the officer and told him to knock off the artificial, tough-guy stuff, that it was not needed in this house; they told him that he was losing the men. But that only seemed to make matters worse. Not surprisingly, the officer did not take such guidance from the men well — it was clear that he thought the whole point of being an officer was that you were above the men and did not have to listen to them. In the end his tenure was a disaster, and he was moved to another house.

Captain Callahan was the exact opposite: His leadership was all by example. He understood the uses of authority in a veteran house — that less was better, that the senior men, even more than the officers, ran the house and set the codes that everyone *had* to respect, because their lives depended on that automatic quality of obedience and loyalty and unwavering commitment at crucial moments. Therefore it was the veteran men who shaped the younger men. If the captain was throwing his weight around, then something was wrong — it meant the senior men were not doing their jobs properly.

One of the things the men came to like about him was his contempt for fire department red tape, of which there seemed to be more and more each year. Those in the upper levels of the bureaucracy had come to be armed in recent years not merely with powerful titles, but also with powerful computers, which they used to generate ever more paperwork and to centralize authority. Callahan was openly contemptuous of some of the bureaucratic byplay, the reports and the paperwork that seemed to make the brass so happy. Those who came to know him believed that this attitude was not merely one of annoyance with the unnecessary work; rather, it was another aspect of his conservative, old-fashioned world view. He disapproved of the trend to grant more and more power to headquarters and less and less to the captains in the firehouses. It had always been in the nature of bureaucracies for the people who ran them to want to centralize power, but now their new electronic machines seemed to give them new leverage in an old struggle.

Late at night, when he was relaxed, Callahan would sometimes talk with a few veteran men in the house about how he felt: that there was far too much micromanaging from headquarters. To the degree that he could circumvent the paperwork, the make-work directives from senior people who had too little to keep them busy, he did. When he got home, he would complain to his wife, Angie, about how much time he spent doing verification of hours put in by his men; by his lights it should have been verified by the all-powerful computers that they loved so much down at headquarters. Just a waste of everyone's time, he would say Callahan also hated the red tape that was increasingly attached to building inspections — if he did a building inspection, he wanted to know only one thing: what it would be like if they had to fight a fire there. That endeared him to the men, who were always wary of an officer who took form more seriously than function.

Still, before they came in with a final verdict, the men wanted one clear test of him under pressure. It came at a fire at St. Luke's Hospital in his first year at the house. It was not a particularly big or dangerous fire, but there had been some hazardous material stored there, and as a result it became the unlikely scene of a test of wills between Frank Callahan and the department brass. For some reason a number of big shots had shown up at the fire — a lot of suit-power, as one of the men noted. When it was over, one of the brass had demanded that Callahan and all his men undergo what was called a washdown — a kind of decontamination process in which not only the clothes of the men were to be cleaned, but also the men themselves. It was an enormous nuisance; had they been proceeding to another fire, it might have been an issue, but their shift was over, and they were on their way home. The personal washdown was a miserable process, one the men truly hated; they would have to go into a tent set up in the street, strip down, and take a cold shower, then dry themselves, probably with paper towels, and wait around, in, at best, some gym clothes, while their own clothes were being cleaned. Callahan was clearly annoyed by the order for his own reasons — it would be an unnecessary imposition inflicted on good men who had just done a tough job, men who were under *his* command. To his mind the order was just about bureaucratic gamesman-

ship and power, not safety. If anyone was supposed to order a washdown for his men, that
person was Frank Callahan.

Callahan looked at the official who had given
the order, technically a superior, and, pointing
out a couple other superiors, including one who
was in charge of all potentially toxic incidents in
the city, he said, "Okay, we'll go through with it,
but I just want you to know that you and your
men walked through the very same halls as we
did, and you were in the same room we were in,
so if my men and I do it, then you do it too, and
we'll damn well watch to make sure you do it."

Then he turned to his company, gathered
right behind him, and he said, "Come on,
Thirty-five Truck, get on the fucking rig and
let's get out of here." Never having stood quite
so tall, the men walked out of the building, got
on the truck, and drove home. Everyone was
thrilled by the moment, and back at the station
house, although Callahan went directly to his
office, the men went upstairs and had their own
celebration: *Hey, we've got us a captain! We've got
us a helluva captain!*

When something went wrong, when some
fireman had not measured up on a particular
fire, Callahan said very little. He would call the
offending man in to his office and give him what
became known among the men as The Look. He
would not say anything in the meeting, just
stare. When The Look had been turned on, time
passed ever so slowly. A few minutes would

seem like an hour. "It was as if he could look right through you and see everything you had ever done wrong all your life, not just the things that you'd actually done, but all the bad things you had ever *thought* of doing — every bad thought you'd ever had," said Sean Newman, a thirty-two-year-old Ladder 35 fireman. Nothing needed to be said — the offender was supposed to know exactly how he had transgressed, and he always did. He was to sit there and ponder his fate and how he had endangered himself and his brothers. Callahan would not dismiss the man, and so he would have to sit there wondering when it was over and when he could leave: In the end, he would have to make that decision for himself, and would finally leave, feeling very small indeed.

The men hated The Look; if only, they thought, he would shout or scream, it would have been easier, they could get the whole incident over with. The Look was infinitely harder to deal with — cold, hard, and unforgiving, seeming to last forever. Later, after his death, when his wife, Angela, came to the firehouse to share her grief with them, the men had asked her if she knew anything about The Look. "Who do you think he practiced on all those years?" she answered.

Callahan's occasional stabs at old-fashioned camaraderie did not work particularly well. There was a roll call once, where he decided to ask some of the men he did not know very well to

42

talk about themselves. "Tell me a little bit about yourself," he asked one fireman. The man in question, duly surprised by this moment of unexpected intimacy from the captain, hesitated for a minute and then answered, "Well, I like to drink a lot. . . ."

If anything bothered Callahan about 40/35, it was the tempo, the fact that they did not have enough fires. Before joining the house, he had been working in ghetto neighborhoods where he would get called on as many as two or three fires a day. So Callahan thought the men at 40/35, especially the younger men, could have used some more work, that it was probably better for a house when there was a great deal more action, because the more runs you did, the better you were, the higher your normal level of concentration, and the more you came back to the station and sat around the kitchen table talking fires, instead of sports and women. As a result, doing things the right way became instinctive.

The Upper West Side was a curious place for Callahan after working for so much of his career in ghetto neighborhoods. The culture of the area was different, so much more affluent. There were all those high-rises, many of them office buildings, which had foolproof high-tech alarm systems that, it would turn out, were not quite so foolproof. The alarms were always tripping accidentally. One day when he was relatively new to the neighborhood, they had gone on a run at a relatively fancy high-rise, and afterward he asked one of the men about a rather elaborate desk in the front of the lobby. "It's the concierge," the fireman answered. What's it for? Callahan had asked. "It's where they leave packages and things," the fireman told him. The captain went home the next day and asked his wife what a concierge was, and whether all apartment houses had concierges. It was, Angie decided, just one more symptom of her husband's culture shock.

Wherever the fire was, though, he was very good at it. Very professional, and very calm. Calm was important; it was one of the most important words in the vocabulary of firemen, and a word they did not use lightly. That and the phrase "do the right thing," as in, "He was the kind of fireman who always did the right thing." Staying calm for a fireman was crucial — for unlike most other peacetime jobs, firemen were in the regular business of the suppression of fear. Every call might be a ticket to a burning inferno where there was no light, where falling walls and ceilings cut off exit routes, where a floor could give out, and where a fireman could become disoriented and begin to feel his source of oxygen failing as he grew weaker and as the heat grew more fierce second by second. Therefore keeping calm was a critical part of the job. Every serious fire could trigger powerful impulses of fear, and if an officer shows that fear on the job, if he is not calm and not disciplined himself, then the fear will spread quickly through the

44

men. Calm is the most basic of the positive words that firemen use to describe one another.

Doing the right thing was equally important. When the men speak of a colleague who does the right thing, they mean he will stay at his post under terrible conditions and not panic. Doing the right thing was going in and risking your life for a trapped civilian or fellow fireman. Firemen define each other by their codes of honor, which, because of the nature of the job, are mandatory and must be instinctive. The men have to be able to count not just on their officers, but on their buddies. Doing the right thing also involves small, seemingly unimportant things in the firehouse. It begins when you are a probie, and it means following certain customs, such as being the first one to the sink to wash the pots and pans after meals. The firehouse, like the military, is based on doing little things right, because if someone does not do the little things correctly, then he probably won't do the big things correctly. Moreover, in a firehouse, if you do not do your share of the routine work, someone else has to do it for you, in which case you pull down the house, and you are a *hairbag*. You do not wait for someone to tell you to do it, you just do it. There is an additional reason: Between moments of fearsome danger, there is often a lot of slack time at a firehouse, and if you do not have codes like this, then it would be very easy for people to become lazy and get in a rut, and for the entire house to lose its sense of cohesion and its purpose.

In the months before the tragedy, Frank Callahan, who was fifty-one years old at the time of his death, had thought about retiring. On occasion he told a few of the senior men that he had checked out his pension numbers and that retirement was a tantalizing possibility. Two of his four children were out of the house, his wife taught school, and they lived reasonably simply in a small town north of New York City. But he felt that the pension needed to be a little bigger. Even more important, when he and Angie talked about it, was the question of what he would do when he retired. Unlike many of the men, who were also plumbers or carpenters or electricians, he did not have a fall-back career, and he thought it was a little late to go back to school for some other degree. So they decided for the moment that he would keep on being a fireman. That was what he did best.

The Callahans rarely took family vacations, but that summer they had decided to and rented a cottage on Lake George, in the Adirondacks. They all went, all, that is, except for Frank, who did not want to go. So Angie and the four children — Harry, Nora, Peter, and Rose — had a great time on the lake, feeling a little guilty that he had stayed home, and that he was, they were sure, almost certainly spending his days watching the History Channel.

Immediately after the first plane, American Flight 11, hit the north tower of the World

Trade Center, Frank Callahan called his twenty-three-year-old son, Harry, who was at his home in Queens. He was concerned that his daughter Nora, a twenty-year-old student at New York University, who worked three days a week in the south tower, for Vestek, might be in the company's seventy-eighth floor offices. But Harry, who was off that day from his job as a mechanic, assured his father that Nora did not work Tuesdays, and that she was not in the building. That had relieved Frank greatly. Then he had called home, which was a little unusual since normally there would be no one at home at that hour — the younger kids would be in school and Angie, who taught eighth-grade math, would be in class. By chance, Rose, thirteen, their youngest child, was home sick. He spoke briefly to her and asked for his wife's phone number at work. Then he called Angie, who was stunned to hear his voice because he almost never called her at work. That threw her, and she knew instantly that whatever had happened was very serious.

By then the second plane, United Flight 175, had hit the south tower. Callahan told her of the attack, that it was the work of terrorists. "It's really, really bad down there. We've just gotten the ticket," he said, "and we're on our way. I've just talked to Harry and Nora is safe." Then he said that he had to hang up because it was time to go. He did not say he loved her, because that was not the way he talked. When the other men at the station later heard about the phone call,

47

they understood that it had reflected not only the totality of his concern, but also his love for his wife: that he had called Angie at work had been his way of showing his love.

Angie had always loved Frank, even if she did not always understand the impulses that made him so quiet and distant. They had met when she was Angela Lang (Irish on her mother's side, German-Swiss on her father's), one of eleven kids in a family that had gone each summer to Breezy Point in Queens, where they had a simple bungalow. The summer colony, located on a sandy spit of land at the western end of the Rockaway peninsula, was popularly known as the Irish Riviera. When Angela was eighteen, she had gone to a party at a volunteer firehouse and she had met this really cute boy with a wonderful mustache. She had picked him up, she said later, and he was very willing to be picked up. He was just out of high school; his father had owned a few bars, but had died when Frank Callahan was about ten. Frank had just taken the firemen's exam when she met him.

Even then he was very quiet. Getting him to talk was, she once noted, not unlike trying to open a safe. When he had first started calling, he would sit silently in the living room, waiting for her. Angie's mother asked her, "Does this guy ever talk?" But if he did not talk a lot, there was something singularly strong, steadfast, and honorable about him. He was a man of substance and determination, uncommon qualities, she felt. She had hoped that as he got older, he would become more open with her and the children, more talkative, but if anything, it went the other way, and she accepted that he was the product of a different, more stoic generation. There had been no role model for him to demonstrate how to talk to his family and how to show emotions or to reveal weaknesses, and his was a background where the two — emotions and weaknesses — were often perceived as being the same thing. He could be as demanding with his family as he was with his firemen. His report card reviews were always serious, not something the four children greatly looked forward to. Each grade from each kid, he seemed to think, should be a little better, because life was a serious place, where the pressures on you were constant, and you *had* to do your best.

Later when Angela spoke of September 11 and of Frank's phone call, she said that he *knew* what he was going into, that they all *knew*. Even without the collapses, she said, he was experienced enough to know that with such big planes hitting towers like that, with all that fuel exploding, that it was going to be the worst thing they ever had faced. They knew, she added, that not all of the men were going to be coming back.

THREE

The chauffeurs on duty that morning, Jimmy Giberson on the truck and Bruce Gary on the engine, were men at the very core of the firehouse. Being a chauffeur meant you had one of the most demanding and important jobs of all: finding the best route to a fire, positioning the rigs so that the men could best work the fire, and for the chauffeur of the engine, managing to find water. Giberson and Gary were both considered absolutely first-rate, and more than any of the officers — officers came and went, and were never a major part of the daily life of the house — the two of them, each in his own way were largely responsible for maintaining the firehouse's traditions and codes. As the saying goes, the men run the firehouse but they are kind enough to let their officers work there.

Both men were always working, both very much aware of setting examples for the younger men. On almost any morning you could look over and see one or the other of them taking two or three hours systematically checking out his rig, making sure that everything worked, leaving nothing to chance; if they left things to chance, the day might arrive when something went wrong, so it was critical to eliminate any mechanical vulnerabilities before the rigs went out. Moreover, the way to insure that things were done right in the house was to set examples by doing things right themselves.

No one wanted to cross them, in part because they were both physically strong, forceful men, but also because of their personal integrity. Both Giberson and Gary had the sheer physical power to dominate others if they so chose. And Gary could do it with his tongue as well. If someone was screwing up, if someone had to be told to help clean up the kitchen or to wash the rig, then Gary would get on him verbally. Giberson, on the other hand, was a quiet man.

Jimmy Giberson was about six feet three inches and 220 pounds, and he was quite possibly the strongest man in the firehouse. He had huge hands and feet. When the men got their boots, a pair would come in one box, but Giberson's feet were so big that each boot came in a separate box. Six days before the terrorist attack, he marked his twentieth anniversary with the fire department. He was thinking of retiring sometime in the next year. As a result, he had started going for overtime, to get his final full year's salary, on which his pension would be based, as high as possible. On the morning of September 11, Giberson, as usual, had come in a little early. He was judged to be an uncommonly talented man in terms of his professional skills, even by the exacting standards firemen use to measure one another. His captain, Jim Gormley, thought him to be the most gifted, natural firefighter he had ever seen. "Jimmy was always in the right spot [or the wrong spot — because it would be the most dangerous one], always instinctively moving to where he should be before you even asked him to," Gormley recalled of him later. But Giberson never tried for an officer's slot, and refused to study for the lieutenant's exam. Gormley had often pushed him to take it, but Giberson had always resisted. He was comfortable as one of the men, absolutely sure he was doing what he wanted, eager for no additional burdens or responsibilities. Giberson needed, Gormley thought, nothing that he did not already have.

Giberson worked all the time — even when he was not at the firehouse. If one of the other firemen needed help with house repairs or renovations, Giberson would invariably show up to help out; he was, among other things, the resident wallpaper specialist. When he hung paper at the home of a colleague, he barely spoke to anyone while on the job and refused any food or drink. Carrying his special wallpaper razor in his teeth, he would do the job perfectly, then, refusing any money he would disappear as politely and as silently as he had arrived.

The sense of inner obligation to the other firemen was particularly strong with him. Once when it was cold out and Mike Kotula was about to go on vacation, Kotula discovered there was too little gas in his car, and the engine, somewhat predictably, would not start. Kotula decided to pour a little gas into the carburetor to prime it, but by mistake he used oil, thereby completely messing up the engine. Giberson not only lent Kotula his car, but while his friend was on vacation, he took Kotula's engine out, broke it down completely, cleaned it, and reassembled it, so it worked perfectly by the time Kotula returned.

Giberson expected that same sense of duty in others. If you were screwing up, he would simply give you a look, and there was no doubt what it meant — that you were cheating on the others, and therefore pulling the house down. Things were to be done right. No one was to endanger himself, or anyone else on a run, and no one was to get even a little sloppy. Matt Malecki was his friend, but one hot summer night Malecki went out on a run without his mask. Giberson jumped all over him — it was a small thing, but Malecki had been careless; no one ever knew whether a run was going to be serious or not, and you *had* to wear your mask. It was not about friendship. Malecki knew not to argue or try to make any excuses. He simply apologized: "Jimmy, you're right and I was wrong," he said.

Giberson was big on tradition. Somehow he always ended up as the principal Christmas party cook, and he took that responsibility very seriously. Starting the night before the party, he would commandeer the kitchen and chase everyone out, unless they were helping him. Then he would do most of the cooking for the 100 people or more who were coming to the party. That was the way it always was, and that was the way it was going to stay.

There was always a palpable sense of Giberson's physical strength. Though the strength went largely unused, the sense was always there. A few years earlier there had been one memorable fight outside a bar frequented by firemen. A man from another house had started getting on Giberson, who just walked away from him and left the bar. But the other fireman followed and kept up the argument. Two blocks away from the bar, the other fireman made the mistake of throwing a punch. Giberson returned it, breaking the man's nose and mashing in his face. Mostly, though, Giberson used the threat of his physical power, rather than the power itself. Once, on a firehouse grocery shopping run, Giberson spotted a man slapping a woman around. Without summoning his pals, he jumped off the rig, caught the man in his enormous arms, and instructed him that this escapade was over, and that it was never — and he meant *never* — to happen again.

That September Bruce Gary, fifty-one, was also thinking about retirement. He had been with the department more than twenty years. His twenty-four-year-old daughter, Jessica, was planning to get married, he said, in June of 2002, and then he was going to go back to plumbing full-time. (He had two other children, Richard, twenty-one, and Thomas, fifteen.) He was a brilliant plumber, which helped him as a chauffeur for the engine, because he *knew* water, and he could always find it. No one doubted that he was going to be able to make a great deal more money as a plumber than as a fireman, but they also thought the firehouse was going to be a very different place without him as its enforcer. He was like the battle-hardened master sergeant in an elite military outfit, someone who made sure that everything worked and worked well.

Gary was of Polish descent, or, as the others believed, he was mostly Polish — nowadays it was hard to tell; people who were supposed to be Irish turned out to be half Italian, and Buddha Arce, who was supposed to be Filipino, was in fact half Filipino and half Irish, while Steve Mercado, who was supposed to be Spanish, was half Puerto Rican and half Irish, or at least a quarter Irish and a quarter German. The name Gary had originally been much longer, it seems, before someone had chopped off several consonants and perhaps even a vowel or two. Gary told the other firemen that once, in the basement of his parents' home, he had come across a trunk, stamped with a name that began with the letters *GARR* and then went on at some length. He had asked his mother whose name that was, and she had answered, "That's *your* name, boy."

Like ethnicity, nicknames were important in the firehouse, and it was part of Bruce Gary's power that he was the house's principal dispenser of nicknames. His own was Slip Mahoney, after one of the tough kids in the Bowery Boys, or Bruce the Bully, a nickname he did not in any way mind, since it implied his power. Everyone else seemed to carry one of his nicknames. Mike Kotula was going through a divorce, so he became Mickey the Lover. Giberson was known as Squarehead, a name he did not seem to like very much but had come to accept, as it was a little late in the game to try to separate himself from it. Another fireman, not known for his speed in picking up the tab at a restaurant or bar when it was his turn to pay, became Skippy Cheap Cheap. Another became Bubble Butt. Gene Szatkowski became Moe, from the Three Stooges. (They already had a Larry — that is, Larry Virgilio.) Someone else, for reasons they could never quite remember, became known as Feta Cheese.

The others were in awe of Gary's sheer physical strength. He was not that tall, perhaps five feet nine or five ten, but he weighed 230 pounds, most of it solid muscle. He had forearms like Popeye's, one of the other firemen noted. He liked to roll up his sleeves and show off his arms; according to his friend Bob Menig, "They looked like nothing so much as four-by-fours." Gary had pushed the others to create a weight room in the house, a decision that at the time had astonished some of the old-timers, who never worked out like he did, and who were a little reluctant to contribute their share of the money for the equipment.

Gary worked out all the time; he could bench-press about 300 pounds. He was also a considerable athlete, a good softball player, a good hockey player, and a good skier, and he was very proud of his athletic ability. Once at the firehouse they had a younger man named Joe Laterza, who was also a very good athlete. He apparently had been a great schoolboy sprinter. But Bruce Gary was not impressed. He claimed he could beat Laterza in a race. No one believed he could — Joe was younger and looked more like a sprinter, but once the challenge was out there, Bruce being Bruce, a showdown was inevitable. So they roped off two blocks on Amsterdam Avenue and held the race. To everyone's surprise save that of Bruce Gary, Gary won.

Gary never let his passion for staying in shape get in the way of his passion for smoking. The other men would ask him how he could take such good care of his body, lifting weights and running the stairs, and then smoke afterward. He would just grunt and tell them that was a dumb question. Not all of the cigarettes he smoked were his own. In fact, Gary was a big smoker of other people's cigarettes, as if by not buying his own packs, he might one day stop. When he hit on another man for cigarettes, he would look at the pack, and if there were, say, only four left, he would observe that since the other fireman was going to need a new pack anyway, he would keep the pack with the four cigarettes.

Gary was, by consensus, the dominating political force in the house. As much as anyone, he was the arbiter of proper and improper behavior, in effect chief justice of his own supreme court, which sat unofficially in chambers in the very kitchen he had expanded with his sledgehammer. If there was a dispute, Gary would dominate it, and his side would always win. He was smart, he was forceful, and on any particular issue he always wanted whatever it was more than anyone else did, so people tended to defer to him. Conversely, whatever he opposed tended not to happen. With Gary, said one fireman, it was his sheer *righteousness* — an odd word, the others added, to apply to a fireman, especially a rough and tough one such as Gary. But if anyone was serious — indeed righteous — about the traditions of the house, about there being a right way and a wrong way to do things, it was Bruce Gary.

Gary had a strong opinion on *everything*, including the food purchased for the firehouse. Regarding cereal, for instance, he would tell the probies fixing breakfast that most cereals were garbage, but if they wanted a *real* cereal, then they should serve up Cheerios. If he traded barbs with the other men, there was always a sense that the repartee was a bit one-sided: He was so forceful a figure that there might as well have been a sign around his neck that said

Don't Mess With Bruce Gary.

Had he, as one younger fireman said admiringly, lived in another time, Gary might have allied himself with Robin Hood, always on the side of justice. Perhaps he would have been Robin Hood's muscle. Gary knew his power and his influence, and he used it shrewdly, always with absolute respect for the firehouse tradition and codes. He had come into the department six weeks ahead of Jim Gormley, and for a long time he had not let Gormley forget that he was senior; he would look at Gormley and say, *"Six weeks,"* and then he would add, "You know, I remember when you were going on your first fire." Gormley eventually left the house, but returned, after nearly ten years, as a lieutenant, and Gary once again delighted in reminding him of the critical difference in their respective seniority — it was six weeks and would forever be six weeks. But when Gormley was promoted to captain in the house, Gary immediately dropped the stinger. That was a line that, for the good of the firehouse, he would not cross. A captain was not to be toyed with or lightly teased — nothing was to be done that might undermine his authority in front of the junior men.

Gary could be very hard on young firemen coming in — testing them constantly, monitoring them for just the trace of the slacker, coming down on them very quickly when he saw signs of weakness or a cheater within. But with Gary it was never harassment for harassment's sake, a veteran beating up on a new kid who was vulnerable and an easy target. It was never for personal advantage — that is, an older fireman leveraging a younger one for better hours or better vacation slots. Rather, it was about conducting a tough, ongoing examination in which he probed the core of the younger man's character, looking for his potential lesser side. It was *always* for the greater good of the firehouse, and it was always about whether the younger fireman was measuring up. That was all Gary cared about.

He was classically a blue-collar guy. He sometimes used big words that he had not yet quite mastered, and a favorite expression of his was to say of something that he did not like or that he feared was a bit trendy, that it was "avant-garde" — which somehow came out as *advent guard.* That was something of a catchall phrase, used to describe anything or any idea that he deemed a little too fancy for the firehouse. He was most wary of younger firemen coming in, as happened more and more, with college degrees; he feared that because they had been to college, they might think they knew more about the job than they did, or that they might believe themselves above the grubbier side of firehouse life, cleaning up after meals and doing the menial support tasks that make a firehouse run efficiently. In addition, he worried they might not have the requisite courage in the face of danger — why should they, if they had other options in life? One of his brothers had gone to college and Gary, known for his exceptional mechanical skills, was famous in his family for telling his brother when some kind of assemble-it-yourself equipment arrived: "Here are the instructions — you take them and read them, and by the time you finish reading them, I'll have the thing put together."

His wariness of college men was well known, and younger men coming into the house were always warned to tread lightly in that area. College guys, Gary clearly believed, had to be taught that they were not a superior species, unless otherwise demonstrated, and therefore they would have to work extra hard before they were accepted. When Sean Newman, a college graduate, joined 40/35 in 1997, he was warned of Gary's prejudice, and told to tiptoe around it. "Hey kid, what did you do before you became a fireman?" Gary asked him. Newman knew it was coming, and he was ready. "I was a sandhog," replied Newman, who then weighed a slight 175 pounds and had in fact worked as a journalist for Reuters. For a moment Gary seemed impressed — the kid was slim but he was a sandhog, and sandhogs were stand-up guys who faced great risks every day to build underwater tunnels, one of the toughest jobs in the city. "There was this very long pause, and then Bruce's eye traveled first to my very soft hands, and then to my pipe-stem arms, and then even he began to laugh. He knew he had been taken if only for a minute or so

— but I got a bit of dispensation," Newman recalled.

A younger man who did not buy into Gary's authority did so at considerable risk. Gary might say of a young fireman who did not meet his standards that the young man would be spending much of his time in the next few months trying to figure out how to get out of a medical pension. Or he might say, "I don't think he's going to be with us very long. Take a good look because you won't see him in a few years." But if a younger man was working hard, Gary would always know, and he would respect that commitment.

Gary knew he was not just a fireman, but a teacher as well; that, by tradition and necessity, it was the responsibility of senior firemen to teach as well as to do. Ray Pfeifer, who weighs well over 200 pounds, remembered catching his first fire with Gary at Fifty-seventh Street and Broadway. Pfeifer was on the nozzle, a physically demanding and scary job — holding the hose and going right smack into the face of fire. He was, he remembered, incredibly nervous that day. Gary was the backup, and he was keeping a sharp eye out on Pfeifer, to make sure that he was all right. After a few minutes of tentative advancing, Pfeifer felt an incredibly strong arm come around him from behind, locking him into position and then lifting him off the ground, as if he weighed no more than a feather. It was Bruce Gary's arm. Slowly and steadily the veteran fireman pushed and carried the nervous rookie into the fire. Gary was utterly calm, and his calm gradually washed over Pfeifer — *If this man is okay, I'm okay,* Pfeifer thought. And then they did it, put out the fire, and Pfeifer took a good long look at the man who had seemed to come out of nowhere to help him. There was a big, cool smile on Gary's face, a smirk almost — the old pro enjoying a new guy's nervousness on his first day. "You did okay, kid," Gary told Pfeifer. "Welcome to the New York City Fire Department."

Lieutenant John Ginley, thirty-seven at the time of his death, was the Engine officer on duty that morning. He had been at the firehouse for three and a half years. Thanks to the television set in the house, the men had, in those early chaotic moments of the terrorist attack, a strong sense of how terrible a day this was going to be. As the news came in, Ginley, as usual, was cool and very much in command. He was, the men later decided, like two different people. The first was the relatively new lieutenant in the house, all business, extremely capable but very quiet — "almost like a priest," one of the senior men said. There was little play to him, almost no lightness when he was at work, and he generally seemed to be outside the usual firehouse games. He was exceptionally precise and well prepared, and yet never out of sync with the job or his men. He seemed young, but his drills were impressive, like those of a true veteran. One of the things that others liked about him was that when he studied, it was not so much for a promotion as to excel at his job. The men, Captain Gormley once noted, were very good at deciding into which category an officer's efforts fell: Was he doing something, pushing himself and pushing them, simply because he wanted to get ahead, or was he doing it because he wanted to do a better job? With Ginley there was no doubt it was always about the latter.

But there was another John Ginley — one the men glimpsed a few times a year at picnics and at the Christmas party. During those times, especially when he was with his two children, nine-year-old Taylor and seven-year-old Connor, he was a completely different man — totally relaxed, all play, and it seemed there was nothing he enjoyed more than his role as a father. That was not surprising, thought Father John Delendick, a priest who was a close friend of the Ginley family and who was named the department's chaplain on September 16, after the death at the World Trade Center of the much-beloved FDNY chaplain Mychal Judge. John Ginley's father, Joseph, was a fireman, and of his children — five sons born within a space of six and a half years — four had become firemen. It was, Reverend Delendick believed, a family in which there seemed to be an unusually tight bond between father and sons, "in which father and sons did *everything* together." Delendick recalled, "In most of the families I knew, when September came, you could feel a sense of relief from the parents because the kids were going back to school, and it was going to be a bit easier and more restful at home with them tied up for most of the day. But with Joe Ginley you could actually sense a very real depression every September — the coming of school meant that he was going to lose his five closest pals, the people he went camping with and played with every day. The fall meant that he had to stop doing most of the things he loved most, with the people he most wanted to be with." Because all her children were boys, Delendick thought, Betty Ginley, who had been born in County Dublin, Ireland, had faced a special challenge in understanding and mastering the world of her family, with its emphasis on sports and masculine activities. Possibly for that reason, she had ended up as a very good golfer, the best in the family.

About an hour and a half north of the city, in upstate New York, Lieutenant John Ginley's wife, April Casey Ginley, was readjusting to the fall routine on the morning of the eleventh. It meant her kids were going back to school and that she would resume her job working for a Japanese cosmetics company. The summer had been an idyllic time for the family, she thought, and it had marked a very good period in her marriage; everyone seemed to be at the same place at the same time. So she was not quite ready for the kids to go back to school, and for the increased pressures of the fall. During the summer they had traveled to Phoenix for a family wedding and afterward had camped near the Grand Canyon for a week; then later in the summer they had gone to Martha's Vineyard and had camped there for about ten days. Although April was not particularly fond of camping, and the weather had not been especially good, they had had a wonderful time. There was no television set, and so everyone had participated in family discussions at night.

John Ginley was in the midst of a twenty-four-hour shift when the first plane crashed into the World Trade Center. He phoned April to tell her to turn on the television set. The engine had not yet been called, he said. She was already watching TV when the second plane hit, and, seeing the sheer magnitude of the explosion, she knew it was serious. She took some solace in the fact that John was probably still at the firehouse, way up on Sixty-sixth Street. There were a million firehouses between Sixty-sixth Street and the World Trade Center, she thought, and even if the men from Engine 40 made a run down to the site, it would take time because Manhattan's streets tended to be clogged with traffic during the day. If John and his men got there, she reassured herself, he would probably be out on the street, doing some form of EMS, rather than in the towers.

John Ginley's next call was to his brother Bob, who was also a fireman, at Engine 307 in

Queens. Four days earlier, on September 7, Bob's son Ryan John Ginley had been born. Ryan was a third son, as Lieutenant John Ginley was a third son, and so this child was his namesake. Before driving to work on Monday, John had stopped by the hospital to see the baby and to visit with Bob's wife, Sue, and they had all noticed that John and Ryan John had the same unusual lines running through their palms. At the firehouse, as the first reports of the attack began to come in, and the tragedy was unfolding on television, John Ginley reached his brother, who was at home in Warwick. "Have you seen the television news?" he asked. Bob turned the set on. He thought John's voice sounded unusually somber, far tighter than usual, very concerned, but somehow determined not to show any unwanted emotion. The only other time Bob had heard it like this was back on Father's Day, earlier in the year, when there had been the explosion at the hardware store in Astoria, Queens, and three firemen had died. John Ginley had called then because he was worried at the time that Bob may have been working that fire.

Now that same tight, controlled tone was in John's voice. "Are you going?" Bob asked his brother. "Not yet," John answered.

Soon after, Bob Ginley left for the hospital to see his wife and new son. Later, when he checked back at John's firehouse, he was told they had left at 9:24. He did the numbers in his head and decided that, with the time it took to go down the normally crowded West Side Highway, and with the south tower collapsing at 9:59 and the north at 10:28, his brother had probably missed the worst of it. As the day wore on and they heard nothing from John, he thought that his brother was simply too busy to call, and he told April not to worry, that her husband was simply overwhelmed by work. But by 5:00, Bob became seriously concerned; it was just too long a time for someone as careful as John not to check in. He kept calling the 40/35 firehouse, and finally he learned that the fireman he had spoken to earlier had gotten it wrong, that the engine had not left the house at 9:24, but instead at 9:08, just five minutes after the second crash. The moment he heard the corrected time, Bob Ginley felt a chill run through him.

Joseph Ginley had never pushed his sons to be firemen, but he had loved his job, and he had always put it out there as a possibility for them; he told them that it was a good life, you lived with other men in genuine camaraderie, and you ended up, almost without realizing it, having the rarest kind of friendships, ones with men who were willing to die for one another. That kind of loyalty was special on this earth. Most important, there was a sense of doing something of value, something that mattered in your community. All in all, Joseph said, it was a very good life, a valuable life, and his sons had witnessed that for themselves, growing up in his home. His boys, Joseph said later, grew up in firehouses, and their childhood photo albums were filled with snapshots of them playing with the men there. The firemen seemed like additional uncles to them.

When Bob and John were still in high school, they talked about becoming firemen, and when Bob was eighteen and a half and John was seventeen and a half, they took the department exam. Their father had suggested that they take the test, because you never knew what you might want to do. Boys of eighteen were not really ready to make final career choices, the father knew, but it would be four years before they gave the test again; by then his sons might want to be firemen, so why not get in line earlier rather than later. They both were working at night as hotel security guards in Manhattan, and they were both already in very good shape — John was a high school quarter-miler who held some local records — but they got in even better shape by running the hotel stairs. They both did well: Bob scored a ninety-eight on the written test and a 100 on the physical; John a ninety-nine on the written, and a ninety-five on the physical. Some 30,000 applicants had taken the test that year, and when the list was posted, Bob was the 426th highest scorer and John, who was a year younger, was around 1,400th on a list of approximately 6,000, of whom about 5,000 eventually became firemen. John went off to college, but nothing that school offered interfered with the strong pull of a career in the fire department.

Reverend Delendick and Joseph Ginley had met at the Anchor Club, a charitable organization of Catholic firemen that was formed in the 1920s to combat prejudices against Irish Catholics in the fire department. Delendick was the chaplain of the group and Ginley was then the president, and in time Delendick officiated at the marriages of four of the Ginley boys and at the christenings of ten Ginley grandchildren. Delendick believed that religion was an integral part of the Ginley home, and that it was directly connected to the boys' desire to become firefighters. The values in the family stressed service and obligation to others; there was a desire to be part of something larger. "In a family like the Ginleys," the reverend said, "becoming a fireman is like living out your vocation — instead of becoming a priest, you become a fireman." As another priest said at one of the memorial services, the fire department can teach you how to put out fires, but they can't teach you the values that are really necessary for the job — the compassion and generosity of spirit, and the willingness to risk your life for others. That has to come from the home and from the religion.

Later, when everyone spoke of John Ginley and the others as heroes making heroes' decisions, April Ginley was not entirely comfortable with the description. What she had always liked about her husband was his modesty and how quiet he was — he was, she believed, the antith-

70

esis of a man who thought he was a hero. There was nothing showy about him, no macho swagger, certainly not at home, and not, she was sure, at the firehouse. She did not think of him as a hero or even for that matter as a fireman; to her, he was a father and husband. What had struck her most was how unusual John was for a man of his background. Old-fashioned and a traditionalist, he was in no way controlling in his relationship with her, as she believed many other traditionalist men tended to be; those men always wanted to make all the decisions for the family because their fathers had made all the decisions for their families. But John had always consulted with her and taken into account what she had felt on any issue that mattered to them as a couple and to their family.

April Casey (who was half Irish and half Italian; her parents, in the more rigidly enforced ethnicity of their day, had been forced to elope) and John Ginley first went out when she was twenty-seven and he was twenty-four. She had been drawn to him because unlike some of the other men she was meeting, he was so quiet and modest, and yet he was still confident and self-assured. She met him with his brother Bob and their friend Steve Milana on Memorial Day weekend in 1988. They passed the day on Steve's boat, and she spent much of the time talking to John. It had turned out to be an unusually pleasant time because he was such a good listener. He had not tried to impress her with his various exploits, but rather he seemed interested in everything about her. She was the one who did the majority of the talking, which was a little surprising because most of the men she knew liked to impress women, and the way they tried to do that was by talking about themselves.

He ended up asking her for her phone number, which she gave him, and which she had already given to his more extroverted friend Steve. She was, she later admitted, slightly shocked at herself for giving out her number to two men in one day. She and John started dating soon thereafter, and when Steve had said something to John about calling her, asking whether John would mind, John had said yes, as a matter of fact, he *would* mind. April had recently broken off an engagement with another young man, and she was still somewhat bruised from that experience. She kept reminding herself, *I don't want to fall in love, I don't want to fall in love.* But then, after about six months of seeing John, she turned to him one night and said she needed to know where this was going and how serious he was.

"Are you asking me to marry you?" he said. He went shopping for a ring, and proposed on Memorial Day, a year after they had met. In 1990, they married.

April remembered the one time John had changed greatly in behavior. It happened around the time of the birth of their first child, Taylor. She had not known what was wrong, and whether or not the drastic change in him was job-related, but there was no doubt something had profoundly changed him. He seemed distant, cold, unable to talk to her, pulled into himself. For the first time, she thought, her marriage might be in trouble; that, perhaps, John was seeing someone else, although somehow that seemed unlikely. Still, a loving man who had always been there for her and open to her was suddenly unreachable.

Slowly the story came out from him. He had been on a fire in the Bronx up around the Grand Concourse and 190th Street, and the Engine had gotten to the fire a little slower than it should have, John believed. He was assigned to the back of an apartment house, and arrived just as a young woman of perhaps eighteen or twenty had panicked and jumped from an upper floor. What made it so painful was that her situation had not been that perilous; she had had more than enough time, if she had held steady. But she was young and scared, and she had not realized there was time to spare, and he had gotten there too late to talk her through it, but just in time to witness her final, desperate decision to jump. If only she hadn't panicked, he kept telling April, if she hadn't panicked, and if only we had gotten there one minute earlier. Just one minute! He could not stop thinking about it, could not get rid of the image of her jumping. April had never seen him so cut off from his normal, optimistic demeanor. Finally, covertly, she called his brother

Bob, hoping that he might have been through a similar experience. She asked him to get John to talk about what had happened. Sure enough, Bob Ginley had been on a fire in which he had had to carry out the burned body of a child, a child they had just missed saving. He reminded his brother that sometimes in this job you did not always get there quite in time. Gradually John Ginley became himself again.

His father, Joseph, had always been aware of the dangers of being a fireman. He had been to the funerals of many firemen killed in the line of duty, and he had taken his boys to a few of them. He had told them of the dangers and that when you chose firefighting as a profession, you had to accept the possibility of losing your life. He himself had almost done so on two occasions — once when he had stayed a bit too long at a fire and had been burned, and another, some twenty-five years ago, when there was a fire in a men's store, and they had been hit with a terrible backdraft. On the latter fire, the lieutenant in charge had had a sixth sense about what was happening and had gotten his men out seconds before the building collapsed. Such incidents were an integral part of being a fireman, Joe Ginley knew. You always understood that there was a very high price that might have to be paid.

On September 11, Joseph and Betty Ginley were halfway across the world, on what had been planned as a long vacation in Asia. They were preparing to depart Seoul for Beijing the next morning, when Joe turned on the television set in their hotel room and saw footage of the planes crashing into the World Trade Center towers. At first he thought he was watching a movie, but then he realized he was watching a real-life tragedy that had been unfolding for some time. One of the CNN anchormen mentioned that it was believed that more than 300 New York City firemen had been lost in the tragedy, and Joseph suddenly felt a terrible fear growing inside him. Eventually he managed to get through to his family back in New York, and he learned that no one had heard from John in many hours. Joseph Ginley knew a great deal about fires and collapses, and he understood right away that unless survivors had been found immediately at that terrible scene, there was very little hope. He was sure then that his son was dead.

FOUR

Kevin Shea was the son of a fireman and brother of a fireman, but he seemed younger and significantly more innocent than the other firemen — he was in no way a macho kind of guy. He was aware that when Steve Mercado, the resident mimic at 40/35, did an imitation of him in the kitchen, he pitched his voice a little higher, but it did not bother him — he had been through all that before at other firehouses, when he was a probie. He knew that in the world of firemen a certain sharp-edged humor such as Mercado's or Gary's was part of the culture. Besides, Shea was uncommonly good looking and finding women was never a problem.

It was not just that Shea had been to college (well, actually, a number of colleges, as he liked to point out: Stony Brook, Emerson, Suffolk, and St. Joseph's in New York), and that he was good at computers — better with them than anyone else in the house. He was just different. Among his colleagues he was known as something of a flake — talented, smart as hell, amazingly hardworking — but somehow *different*. It was a description he would not necessarily have

76

disagreed with. A few years earlier, before he had joined the department, unsure of what he wanted for his future, he had taken the exam for the police department, and he had done reasonably well. But there was a moment when he was hooked up to a lie detector machine and was asked questions about himself, and, in his own words, he had folded. One of the questions was whether he had ever stolen anything. He thought long and hard about the answer, scanning in his mind his whole autobiography going all the way back to early school days, and he answered, "What about paper clips?" No, the interrogator said, somewhat annoyed, he meant stealing something of consequence — paper clips did not count. Well, Shea answered, I stole some magazines once. That, if anything, annoyed the interrogator even more, which in turn threw Shea off. By the end of the session, he managed to confuse both himself and the machine, and to irritate the cop who was doing the questioning. It convinced Shea that he was not cut out to be a cop, a verdict, he was sure, that the officer testing him agreed with.

He was still quite new at the firehouse, still finding his way around, still trying to prove himself to the officers and the senior men. He had not yet figured out Captain Callahan. There was always that distance to the captain, which to the older men was merely a sign that the captain was being the captain, but to the newer men, especially someone like Shea, it seemed more personal. And there was the fact that Callahan had a somewhat weird sense of humor. He liked to test people, quizzing them with questions to which it was hard to get the right answers. "How much do you tip a bellboy?" the captain once asked Shea, who puzzled over the answer, for he had not tipped that many bellboys in his young life. Finally, he answered, "Five dollars." Callahan shook his head, showing that the answer was wrong, and then he said, "Find out what it is, and let me know when you know." That had left Shea even more puzzled.

Shea grew up in Brooklyn and then on Long Island. When he had been allowed to choose his firehouse, he knew he wanted one in Manhattan, because he considered it the most sophisticated borough, and by working there, he was sure that he would become more sophisticated. When he called Captain Callahan, to tell him of his decision, the captain seemed surprised and asked him why. "Other houses are much busier," Callahan pointed out. But Shea insisted he wanted this one — he was sure he would learn more about all aspects of life there.

He joined the house on July 3, 2001, arriving very early in the morning that day, around 3:00 a.m., determined to make a good impression. He was carrying with him all kinds of food, some things he had made, such as strawberries dipped in chocolate, and all the fixings for an egg-white omelette that he intended to make for his fellow firemen. No one who was awake seemed very interested in eating at that moment, but later, when they went on a run, Shea started cooking, and by the time they returned, around 6:00, they were all hungry, and the meal was a success.

Shea and Bruce Gary were not exactly a natural fit, but Gary always spoke well of the young fireman, for Shea worked maniacally hard — harder than almost anyone other than Buddha Arce, who was widely regarded as the hardest working young man in the house's recent history. Shea's nickname for a time was Ricochet (or Rick O'Shea) because he moved around the firehouse so fast. What Gary particularly liked about Shea was that when he made coffee in the morning, he did not simply prepare one big pot and try to make it last too long, but, because coffee gets bitter when it sits, Shea would make it fresh five or six times each morning. At 7:00 a.m. Gary might have his first cup of coffee, and he would tease Shea: "This tastes old, like six-thirty coffee."

"No, no," Shea would say, "it's *six-forty-five* coffee."

"You absolutely sure about that?" Gary would say. "It tastes more like six-thirty than six-forty-five."

Most of the men in the house had other jobs — they were plumbers, or carpenters, or mechanics — and Shea had one, but it was typically quite unfireman-like: He entertained at children's parties by impersonating Big Bird, a Ninja Turtle, Barney, or Elmo. This did not entirely please Bruce Gary, who thought it somehow beneath a fireman's dignity to dress up in goofy costumes. "We can't have someone from this house going as Daffy Duck or Barney," Gary told him. *"A fireman dressing up as a purple dinosaur!* Jesus! You've got to go as a hero."

"What about if I go as Spiderman," Shea asked, and Gary said, yeah, that was better — Spiderman was all right, a lot better than Barney. And so Shea worked a few parties as Spiderman, and in time showed up dressed as the superhero at the firehouse picnic for the benefit of everyone's kids.

Shea had just been relieved when the first call had come in on September 11. He was loading his personal gear into his car, parked across the street. He tried to get on the Truck, his usual assignment, but all the seats were taken. So he went to the office of the Engine, where Lieutenant Ginley was working, and asked if he could go with the Engine. Ginley said they hadn't been called yet, but he gave Shea permission to join them if they were.

Shea was still taking care of his gear when the Engine got the call. That was, he remembered, almost immediately after the second plane hit. At this point, Shea put on his gear and he took his video camera with him. His account remains the only record of what happened on either the Truck's or the Engine's rides down, because he was the only survivor of the thirteen men who went out from 40/35; his account is fragmentary because of the injuries, both physical and emotional, he suffered that morning, including a severe concussion. Much of Kevin Shea's recall of what actually happened at the site remains clouded.

On the ride down, Shea sat next to Mike D'Auria, the twenty-five-year-old probie who had not even graduated from the academy yet. This was only D'Auria's second real fire. They got to the site amazingly fast, Shea thought. Normally the traffic in midtown Manhattan tended to slow the rigs down, but this morning they moved practically unimpeded down the West Side Highway as if somehow everyone had known in advance that something terrible would happen and had stayed clear of the highway. As they were riding, Shea was thinking, two planes, two towers, that had to be the work of terrorists, and he asked Lieutenant Ginley if he thought it was terrorism. "It appears to be so," Ginley said, "but we just don't know yet."

Mike D'Auria was a quiet man, and in that way the antithesis of Shea, who was always talking. Shea tried to engage him in conversation but D'Auria seemed very much inside himself. Shea knew how hard it must be for the probie, so young and so inexperienced, traveling toward so dangerous a site. Shea knew that Steve Kelly, one of the senior men at the house, thought D'Auria was unusually reflective and sensitive, somewhat different from many of the firemen. D'Auria read widely, Kelly had said, and there

81

was a deep, spiritual sense to him — almost all of his reading was about his own spiritual quest.

Kelly's was an interesting endorsement. He came from a tough part of Yorkville, a neighborhood on the Upper East Side of Manhattan, and he often spoke of how thin a line there was between the kids he grew up with who became firemen and cops, and those from the same streets who ended up in prison. He was not entirely comfortable with the more raucous side of the firehouse, and he had liked Mike D'Auria from the start. They not only seemed to feel the same way about things, but Kelly sensed that he and D'Auria were struggling with the same issues, trying to figure out what a good life was — that is, a moral and spiritual life. What was the guiding purpose of a human life? To what should one dedicate oneself? They read many of the same books, and Kelly was impressed that D'Auria had read Carlos Castaneda, the cult writer who had explored Mexican and Native American shamanism and whose works were not exactly firehouse best-sellers.

Kelly knew his own life might have easily been a complete disaster, and yet he had somehow managed to save himself and was doing something he wholeheartedly believed in. College had never been a possibility for him — he was street-kid, not college-boy material. Becoming a fireman had given him dignity and pride. He now saw some of that same background in Mike D'Auria, although D'Auria, he was sure, had never come as close to slipping through the cracks as he had.

Kelly thought that he and D'Auria had a chance to become very close friends in the years ahead. Unlike many of the other young men who came to the firehouse from blue-collar neighborhoods in Brooklyn, Queens, or Staten Island, D'Auria did not bring with him all the usual neighborhood prejudices about people who were different. In fact, D'Auria seemed to have almost no prejudices at all. Part of it was the influence of his mother, Nancy Cimei D'Auria Marra, who hated the ethnic biases that she had grown up among. She had in the past, she often noted, argued with her own parents about what she thought were their prejudices.

Part of it as well, Kelly was sure, was the fact that D'Auria had worked in several restaurants, and New York's restaurant kitchens were often the first stop for many of the city's newest residents moving north from the southern part of the hemisphere, who worked there as dishwashers and busboys. Many of them had come from impoverished Third World countries, and they had no green cards, and were thus working illegally. D'Auria had seen how difficult their lives were — how hard they worked, and how vulnerable they were to everyone and everything around them (especially to the people who employed them) — and he had come to admire their inner strength, their courage, and their optimism.

That weekend D'Auria had helped cook several of the meals at the firehouse, a job that he loved and a role the other firemen loved to see him play, because he alone among them was a genuine chef. D'Auria had gone to cooking school after high school and had apprenticed at several excellent Manhattan restaurants. When he cooked at the firehouse, there was always a crowd of five or six men, trying to watch and learn, around him. He had promised that he was going to teach them the five classic sauces, upon which all the other ones are based, that every chef has to know.

D'Auria was about to start work as the pastry chef at a restaurant he and some friends were going to open soon in Staten Island. The new job, he was sure, would knit perfectly with his firehouse hours. One of the restaurants he had worked at was Gabriel's on West Sixtieth Street in Manhattan, just a few blocks from the firehouse. It was a popular place in the Lincoln Center area, and he had done well as a grill man there. Because he was well thought of at Gabriel's — there was a job for him there anytime he wanted it — he had gone back there the Friday before the tragedy to sharpen the firehouse knives; he did not want to bring his own, professional-quality knives to the house, because if he took them home with him at night, as any restaurant chef does, it might look impolite, as if he was violating the communal sense of the firehouse.

D'Auria had been associated with 40/35 since July and he loved it there, because the senior men had not exploited his status as a probie. Instead they had worked hard to teach him how to be a fireman. Still, for quite a while he had remained frustrated because his tour lacked an actual fire. Week after week he went to work, and there was no action, though on the days he was off, there seemed to be frequent fires — thirteen, in fact, as he told his mother, and *none* when he was on.

He was still single and lived in Staten Island with his mother, her second husband, and his grandparents. Sometimes after he finished a shift at the firehouse, he would have breakfast with his mom. "Anything yet?" Nancy Marra would ask. "Not yet," he would answer. Then finally, in the middle of August there was a fire, not a huge one to be sure, just a small kitchen fire. But the other firemen had let him be the nozzle man, and he had put it out. He returned to the station house absolutely triumphant. "I finally got my fire," he told his mother the next day.

Nancy Marra agreed with Steve Kelly that her son was somehow different and special. She had often pondered why. He was, she knew, serious about finding a spiritual path in life, and yet, in the traditional sense, he was not religious. When he was a boy, she had *never* been able to get him to go to church. Yet he was only eleven years old when a group called the Guardian Angels became popular in New York as a kind of vigi-

85

lante force trying to reduce crime. Michael had been fascinated by them and had decided that he was a de facto Guardian Angel. He started to patrol his school yard, on the lookout for any instances of bullying, until the school principal called Marra and said that her son had to stop — he did not think it appropriate for an eleven-year-old to act as a self-appointed playground policeman.

D'Auria never lost the idea that he had to assume responsibility for the people around him. When he was barely twenty, he was working as an apprentice in a restaurant kitchen, and a friend also working there was having trouble with drugs and had gotten his girlfriend pregnant. When D'Auria found out, he took off his expensive watch, gave it to his friend, and simply told him he had nine months to straighten out his life, adding, "And every time you look at that watch, I want you to think of how much time you have left to get yourself clean."

Later, long after it was clear that he had died in the disaster, his mother was still trying to figure out what it was that had set him apart. It was then that Nancy Marra found an essay about her son that her nephew Robert Perretta had written for a grammar-school assignment. The students had been asked to portray someone they knew, and Perretta had decided to write about his favorite relative: "He is a good and holy man. He thinks no one should have a bad life. He never hates anyone, and thinks everyone should have a good life. He respects other people and he respects himself." How odd, she decided, that an eleven-year-old should get it so exactly right.

One thing that both Nancy Marra and Steve Kelly understood was that Mike D'Auria was very serious about his tattoos and that they were in their own way quite revealing — he did not, as was often the case, sport the names of loves past and present or various symbols of American patriotism. Instead, on one arm he had the Serenity Prayer: "God grant me the serenity to accept the things I cannot change, the courage to change the things I can, and the wisdom to know the difference between the two." He also had on that arm a tattoo of Saint Anthony, the patron of lost things. On the back of his right shoulder, there was a tattoo of Saint Michael, the archangel, which his mother believed he put on because he had wanted a protector. He had been planning a tattoo for his other arm, and he had wanted to put a Native American leader there. He and Steve Kelly had discussed which chief he should choose, and Kelly had pushed for Chief Joseph of the Nez Percé, but there was also some talk of Sitting Bull.

On Monday, September 10, D'Auria had worked a regular shift with his close friend Donald D'Amelio, who was also a probie at 40/35. D'Amelio was a year older than D'Auria, and he too was single. They had become buddies their first day together at the academy, two young

87

men from similar backgrounds with similar dreams. D'Amelio liked to say later that they could finish each other's sentences. At the academy, they had often teased each other about their bright futures in the department. "I can't wait to see you in ten years when you're running the whole show," each would say to the other. That Monday evening, they got off work at 6:00 p.m. and went to The Saloon, a restaurant across from Lincoln Center. There they grabbed a bite and spoke quite candidly about the risks involved in their work; it was the kind of conversation that very young firemen sometimes have with each other, but dared not have with the veteran men, lest it be taken as a sign of timidity or fear.

D'Amelio was in a good mood that night, but he was bothered by the challenge of what they were doing and how hard it was, how much there was to learn and how quickly they had to learn it. After all, their lives were on the line. Midtown, with all its high-rises, was singularly difficult. Every building was different, and yet when you went in as a fireman, you had to have some sense of what these different buildings were like. You couldn't get it on the spot because there was usually so much smoke that the visibility was poor, and the pressures to respond under crisis conditions were immense. There had been a fire recently that they had not caught, but the other men had told them about. It had been in a duplex, and when the men had arrived, they had found the apartment filled with smoke. The place had, it turned out, a sunken living room, but the smoke had obscured it. Unable to see the floor, a couple of the men, including Captain Callahan, had fallen down. Midtown Manhattan, with its many architectural styles and idiosyncratic buildings, was filled with ambushes like that, D'Amelio pointed out to D'Auria. It was terribly dangerous, and it was their job to know the specific dangers. He was feeling frustrated because there was so much to learn, and yet he felt he knew so little at this point.

But D'Auria told his friend that they could not afford to worry about the risks — if they thought too much about them, they would never be able to do their job. They had to think only of their mission, he insisted, and their mission was to save lives. You could not be governed by fear. Saving lives, that's all I'm in it for, D'Auria said. Then they talked briefly about death, and D'Amelio said that burning to death was not a way he wanted to go. But D'Auria said he was not worried about that; he was sure that if he died, it was going to be in something big. "What! Are you going to die in World War Three?" D'Amelio teased him.

After dinner Mike D'Auria went with D'Amelio to Brooklyn to watch the *Monday Night Football* game, and when it was over, D'Auria caught a cab back to the firehouse, so he would be there on time for the mutual he was doing for Bob Menig, who had to leave the firehouse in time for his doctor's appointment. On the morning of September 11, Michael D'Auria had been a firefighter for all of eight weeks.

Nancy Marra had slept badly that Monday night and had gotten up late on that Tuesday morning, after 9:00 a.m. Her husband, Bill Marra, told her that two planes had hit the World Trade Center. She had asked him if he thought Michael would be working there, and he had answered that he certainly thought Michael would be there, seeing as he worked in mid-Manhattan. At first Nancy had not been that worried, but they lived right across from the local school and by mid-morning she saw all the kids being let out and the parents coming to pick them up. It was then that she began to understand the magnitude of the disaster.

It was her time to start worrying — even though Michael had always said, "Mom, stop worrying — you worry too much." Of course that just made her worry even more. (To the degree that his family was a firefighting family, it was from her side, the Cimeis, of whom there were nine members in the extended family who were firemen.) She watched the mounting horror that morning, and when the second tower fell, it seemed especially eerie, as if she were watching some kind of replay of the first collapse, rather than another real collapse, taking place live. She kept thinking to herself: *Am I really sitting in my living room, watching this?* For some reason she did not think Michael was in that much danger, and around 10:30 a.m. her sister Angela Perretta called to say that she had seen Michael on television and he had been helping people get out of the building. That had been reassuring, because apparently the sighting took place after the buildings had come down.

But then time passed, and there were no calls from him. By then much of the family had gathered at her house, and she decided that they had to go on as if nothing was wrong. Michael will call, she had told everyone, and she went ahead and cooked dinner — pasta with a tomato and prosciutto sauce. A place was set for Michael. It was only when dinner was over, and she had put his full plate back on the stove, that the symbolism of the act struck her. Suddenly she could no longer control herself, and she burst into tears. For the first time she permitted herself to understand that perhaps he was not going to be coming home.

Mike D'Auria was not the only person on the Engine who was silent during the ride down. What struck Shea was how quiet everyone was. The only conversation came from Lieutenant Ginley and Bruce Gary, who were on the radio to their superiors, and then talking to each other, trying to decide where to put the Engine. Shea had a sense that the veterans were so quiet because they all knew something that he did not. Nevertheless, Shea knew that this run was different from anything he had gone on before.

As they got nearer and nearer the site, Shea remembered, he saw a lot of smoke and a hole in one of the towers where one of the planes had hit. He saw cars on fire because they had been hit by falling debris. And then he saw people jumping from the buildings, and he heard the thud of their bodies as they hit the pavement — a sound he would never forget.

When they got there, there was mass confusion. The destruction of the city's Emergency Command Center in 7 World Trade Center had the effect of cutting off the nerve center for the fire department. Communications were terrible, and there was a good deal of uncertainty about what their orders were. They were waiting about 200 feet from the south tower, and Shea was carrying a Purple K extinguisher, which was used to fight fires involving airplane fuel — though these extinguishers were ridiculously inadequate for the massive amount of fuel that drove this fire. While they waited, Shea got out his camera and started videotaping the scene, thinking it might eventually make a good training film. Then the men got their orders to move in. Lieutenant Ginley led them toward the south tower lobby, and Shea was a few feet behind the others because he had been putting his camera away. Ginley had given him permission to look for his brothers from Ladder 35, his usual assignment. What the Engine was going to do was problematic at this point because it probably wasn't going to be able to do anything with water.

The morning of the tragedy Marion Otten, whose maiden name was also Otten, which made her technically Marion Otten Otten, was getting her kids ready for the school bus in Islip, Long Island. Because the bus was usually right on schedule, her eyes were rarely far from the clock at that time of the morning, and so she remembered that it was exactly 8:46 a.m. when her husband, Michael, called from the firehouse to tell her to turn on the television set. "Why?" she asked.

"Because a plane has just crashed into one of the World Trade Towers," he said. "Where is your brother?"

Her brother, also named Michael Otten, worked at the World Trade Center. "I think he's in Tower Two," she said. Indeed he was, working for Mizuho Capital on the eightieth floor of the south tower. "I need to go. I've got to get the boys on the bus," she told him, referring to their three sons, Christopher, eleven, Jonathan, eight, and Jason, five. "I'll talk to you later."

Marion's husband, forty-two-year-old Michael Otten, the son and grandson of firemen, was at the firehouse that morning working a twenty-four-hour shift. That was a break from his usual routine, which was to get up at 5:30 a.m. and be out the door by 5:45, in order to make a ninety-minute commute — he would shower and eat his breakfast at the firehouse. The commute was about as long a commute as one could reasonably make, and it was hard for Michael. A firehouse in Queens or Brooklyn would have been far easier for him, but he had no desire to transfer. Often Otten would drive in with Ray Pfeifer, who lived nearby and was his closest friend in the house.

Marion Otten finished putting the boys on the bus and then went back into the house, just in time to see the second plane hit. Her husband, whom she would soon start referring to as My Michael, in order to differentiate him from her brother, had not been scheduled to work that day, but he was doing a mutual for one of the men, who was getting married in a few weeks and who needed to prepare for the wedding. In addition, Michael Otten had relieved another fireman early that morning and sent him home, so that in subsequent weeks when Marion saw the other fireman, he had great trouble looking at her, and he would say things like, "If I could change places with Mike . . . if I could only manage to switch places with him."

At first it was her brother Michael whom Marion worried about. She tried calling her sister-in-law and her mother, but there was no one at home. It was a morning of frantic phone calls all over the city, and it was difficult if not impossible to get through to anyone. Michael, who was thirty-five, had lived through the first World Trade Center attack eight years before.

When the first plane struck the other tower on September 11, Michael had heard a terrible noise, and like everyone else, ran to the window, and saw great clouds of smoke pouring from a giant gash in the north tower and what seemed like millions of pieces of paper flying out. The managing director of his firm, Yuji Goya, was already in command, telling everyone, "Get out! Get out!" Otten went to get his cell phone and briefcase, but Goya screamed at him, "Forget it. Get out!"

Michael Otten made it to the stairwell, already filling up with people from the floors above them — everyone, he thought, was behaving very well and the exodus was surprisingly orderly. He had gotten down to the forty-sixth floor when they heard an announcement saying everything was okay, they could continue out, or go back to their offices. There was an express elevator on the forty-fourth floor, which went back to the seventy-eighth, and most people seemed to be crowding onto it. Otten wondered what to do. Even as he was deciding, the elevator took off for the upper floors. About three or four minutes later it returned. Otten decided to get on, but the elevator was so crowded that the door would not close: It was blocked by a young man's backpack. Again and again the backpack blocked the door. Michael was about to ask the young man to move farther into the elevator, just as the second plane hit their tower. The explosion was immense, like nothing he had ever heard or felt before. He remembered the walls of the elevator began to collapse inward, and he was suddenly terrified that the elevator itself would go into a free fall to the bottom of the shaft. Everyone managed to get off. There was debris everywhere, and for a time it was hard to see. The building seemed to move three or four feet, swaying back and forth; Otten had to reach out to the wall to prop himself up and to keep from falling.

Gradually the air cleared, and Otten made it to the stairwell again. He was once again surrounded by people moving with purpose, and with no one openly panicking. It was hard to judge time in that environment, Otten thought, but he believed that he made it down from the forty-fourth floor to the ground level in about five minutes. As he reached the lower floors, he had one last image, of descending with the others and the firemen coming in, single file alongside them, heading in the opposite direction, up into the tower. He looked to see if he could find his brother-in-law, but he could not.

As they reached the lobby, there were men who were obviously very much in charge, risking their own lives while giving directions, telling them where to go, telling them to *Hurry up, move along, keep going, and don't look up!* Of course, Otten remembered, they all looked up and saw the apocalyptic sight — the tower burning, the debris falling, a terrible vision from an unimaginable nightmare. He and two friends from his office made it out, and started zigzagging away from the building: a block north, a block east, a block north, a block east, until they were safe. They tried calling loved ones on their cell phones, but all the circuits were blocked. It was not until they finally reached an office building about twenty blocks away from the World Trade Center, where they were able to use phones with landlines, that they were able to reach their families and tell them that they were all right. Around 11:00, Marion heard that her brother had gotten out safely.

Later, as he replayed in his mind what had happened, Michael Otten decided that his had been a terribly close call and that he had been saved by Yuji Goya, his managing director, who lost his own life saving others, by the young man with the unwieldy backpack, and, he believed, by his brother-in-law Michael Otten and men like him who had given their lives for utter strangers.

The five men from 40/35 who had gone to Ocean City, Maryland, for a golfing holiday had passed an ebullient Monday evening, some of them imbibing enthusiastically at a local bar. They had slept a little late the next morning, but then Mike Kotula got a call on his cell phone from his son, who said that a plane had hit the World Trade Center. At first they thought it was a small plane that had strayed into the tower, but then they watched the story unfold on television, and they knew immediately how bad it was. So they piled into the car and raced back to New York. It was the fastest ride he had ever taken, Kotula remembered later, and the slowest as well. It was deathly silent inside the car — not a word was spoken the entire way back. They drove at about 100 miles per hour, and they listened to the news on the car radio, trying to imagine what their pals were going through, trying to convince themselves that the 40/35 rigs had gotten down to the site late enough so that the men were outside, helping to rescue people. That was the key word: *outside.* But they also knew their hope was not anchored in any real information, and the news on the radio was becoming grimmer and grimmer. By the time they got to New Jersey the radio broadcaster was announcing the collapse of the south tower.

From every corner of the city and its surrounding communities the men from 40/35 who had not been on duty that morning were making their way to the firehouse and to Ground Zero, as it was already being called. It wasn't easy to travel in the city by this point — public transportation was down and there were roadblocks everywhere — but somehow they got to the site, whatever it took. Terry Holden, the house's senior fireman, came in from suburban New York, driving off the highway at times to bypass traffic, using the grass shoulders along the Palisades Parkway. When he got to the firehouse, he found it in total chaos. Some officers were trying to assign the men to teams, but it was unusually disorderly because of the breakdown in communications at the upper level of the chain of command. (One of the things the senior firemen were privately very angry about was the outdated quality of firehouse communications gear — hardly up to speed. They believed that it had *never* been good enough, especially during high-rise fires, and that in the case of the World Trade Center, with the central nervous system knocked out, better communications equipment might have saved a large number of firefighters, particularly before the second collapse.)

The men assembling did not think they were moving quickly enough, and there was virtually a mutiny; some of the men were so restless and angry that they began to commandeer vehicles, anxious, if need be, to go down on their own. Others hitched rides. Some ran on foot, and one or two biked down. By the time most of them got there, Holden remembered, the two towers had collapsed, and it was essentially impossible to do any rescuing. They were pushed back by the firemen who had gotten there earlier, and who feared that more buildings might fall. It was no longer a question of how many men they might save, Holden later remembered thinking, but of not losing any more.

To the degree that they could, the rescue workers from 40/35 worked the edges of the ruins, shouting the names of their colleagues and stopping everyone they met to ask if they had heard or seen anything of the men from Engine 40 or Ladder 35. Sean Newman, one of the first of the 40/35 off-duty men to get there, at around 10:30, knew immediately that the news was going to be very bad. Everywhere he went, he asked other firemen if they had seen or heard anything about the men from his house. But no one knew anything. In time he found the rigs, but by then he was already so aware of the completeness of the tragedy that he could not bring himself to look alongside the officer's seat, where a list of the men who had gone on the run was kept — he did not want to see the names of his friends and colleagues who had been caught up in this terrible day and who he feared might all be dead. He did, however, see a giant shoe where the chauffeur of the truck had sat, and he knew that it meant that Jimmy Giberson had been driving, because in the house, only Giberson had feet that big. He knew as well that it meant that they had almost surely lost Jimmy.

Terry Holden had never seen anything like this wreckage before. Usually if there was a collapse, it was possible to dig through it to some of the pockets, known as voids, in which the firemen might have survived. But this chaos was so enormous; it was an avalanche of steel and concrete that had fallen straight down. The weight of the collapsed material was beyond Holden's comprehension. It was hard to look at this and think of anyone living through it. Firemen like to think that their will and their talents are great enough to fight back against the awesome force of even the worst fire. But no one could imagine challenging this collapse and rolling it back. There was not going to be much in the way of voids, Holden thought.

Chris Lynch, a chauffeur on the Engine who had worked the Monday night shift, had just missed going on the run. He had been relieved by Bruce Gary, who told him to go home early. Lynch, thirty-six, had wanted to make the 9:15 train from Penn Station to Farmingdale in Long Island, where he lived. The next train was not until 10:15, so he could save an hour by taking the early train. Lynch called his wife to tell her that Gary had relieved him, that he was going to make the early train, and to ask if she could meet him at the station. Just then, as Lynch was in the office talking to his wife, both Steve Mercado and Gary came over to tell him that he should call Battalion because they might be looking for someone to work at another house. He would be able to pick up some overtime that way. Lynch was coming off a fifteen-hour night shift (the day shifts are nine hours), and he had a twenty-four-hour shift coming up the next day. He had already worked a good deal of overtime in the preceding weeks, and so he decided not to call in to Battalion.

Instead he rushed over to Penn Station and made it in time to catch his train. Minutes prior to his boarding, the first plane hit the north tower, and as the train passed under the East

River to Queens, the conductor made an announcement about it. He was somewhat casual, so the news did not seem so urgent to Lynch at first; he thought that a small plane had collided with the building by accident. Then very quickly the passengers began to pick up more bulletins, among them that a second plane had hit the other tower. Shortly before 10:00, a woman with a Walkman said that a plane had crashed into the Pentagon. By then Lynch knew that it was a terrorist attack. He continued home to Farmingdale, changed and showered, and got ready to go back to work. For some reason, he did not think immediately of his own company going down there — "It didn't dawn on me. It should have, but it didn't," he said later. With his wife uneasy and obviously frightened about the idea of his return, he quickly ate a sandwich, headed back to the city, and raced to the firehouse. The rigs were gone; what he found instead was complete chaos. So Lynch and a few others grabbed a Red Cross van and headed to Ground Zero.

At the site Lynch wandered through the rubble looking for his friends. Finally he ran into another member of the house and asked him, "Have you seen anything of our guys?" The answer was so stark that he would never forget it. "They're all dead," the other fireman said. Lynch thought, *Are you crazy? That just can't be. Nothing like that's ever happened before. If it's bad, maybe we lose one or two men. So it can't be, things like that don't happen. You have to be wrong.* But then the other man's words began to sink in, and he began to wrestle with the terrible questions that would haunt so many of the men who had not been on the rigs that morning: Why did *I* survive? Why was *I* allowed to live?

That night when he finally got home, Chris Lynch was in his bathroom, a bathroom that Bruce Gary had been renovating for him — at no cost, of course — and there he saw written on the unfinished plywood wall Bruce's notes to himself what he needed, what he wanted to do, measurements, and his cell phone number, just in case Chris needed to call him.

When Ray Pfeifer, one of the men from the Maryland golf outing, arrived at the World Trade Center site, among the first people he ran into was Thomas Von Essen, then New York's fire commissioner. Pfeifer asked him what he had heard, how bad it was. "About five hundred," Von Essen answered, and it took a second for that to register, for Pfeifer to realize that Von Essen was way ahead of him in estimating casualties and that 500 meant 500 firemen presumed missing.

And so it began for Ray Pfeifer, his struggle with something new to him, trying to comprehend both the scope and the permanence of this tragedy, the idea that this was a nightmare he would never wake up from. It was never going away, and nothing was ever going to be the same for him. It was not a new chapter in the book of his life, it was more like a new book for his life.

Back at the firehouse, there was a darkening sense of what was happening, of how terrible it was, a tragedy beyond anyone's comprehension. By the early afternoon, there was talk that the department might have lost more than 300 men. Most of those gathering back at Sixty-sixth Street — many of them sent in from other houses — knew all too well from watching television and seeing both buildings pancake down that this collapse was likely to have been fatal to anyone under it. Gradually, there was a strong sense that the unthinkable had happened, that every man they had sent down from 40/35 might have died. Throughout the day, there were more and more reports, and the news was unrelentingly bad. Not only had their own men probably been lost, but also a number of other firemen with exceptionally close ties to the firehouse, men who still palled around with the 40/35 men: Larry Virgilio, who had worked there for years before going over to Squad 18 (a special unit committed to dealing with hazardous materials); Mike Boyle and David Arce, the boyhood friends who had become firemen together and, even after moving on to Engine 33, still played on the 40/35 softball team; and Larry Stack, a big strapping man of about six feet four inches who had served as a lieutenant at 40/35 in the early '80s, and had worked there as well as a covering captain when one of the house's regular officers was either sick or on vacation. Stack was widely regarded by the men as an almost perfect officer, balancing an instinctive sense of command with just the right amount of warmth, which he always seemed to summon at just the right time. Slowly it dawned on everyone that they were witnesses to, and part of, the worst day in firefighting history.

One of the genuine heroes who emerged at 40/35 that day was Mike Kotula, who had been among the men playing golf in Maryland. On his return, Kotula had joined the others from the house in the search for their buddies at Ground Zero, and he saw at once how hopeless it all was. Trying to find anything under that grotesque mountain of rubble had been more than he could bear. So it was that when he got back to the firehouse around midnight on Tuesday, he had begun almost purely by instinct to man the phone, taking the incoming calls from the wives and families and closest friends. He had done it in part because he could not bear to go back down to Ground Zero, but he had also done it because he believed that someone who knew and loved all these men and their families should be on the phone — this was not a job for a stranger.

His new task was in those heartbreaking hours and days very important, and he stayed on the phone, almost without a break, through Saturday night. Early on, he had taken a brief break to eat while one of his colleagues manned the phone. Just then, the daughter of one of the missing men called in for her hourly update, and she was upset that Mike was not there to field her call. With that, he did not leave the phone until Sunday morning. Other men brought him food and coffee, and he worked through the night, for the vigil never ended, nor did the incoming calls. Somehow it was decided, without ever being decided, that Kotula was very good at this, and therefore he should stay on phone duty as long as he could handle it. Kotula was aware that in the very first hours after the attack, some newcomers to the house had handled the phone and had, because of their own inadequate sources, passed on erroneous information — including the wrong departure times for the rigs, which had given families perhaps too much hope early in the crisis.

Now it was Kotula's very delicate job to deal with the appalling truth — that there was almost no hope for anyone — and to do it in a humane way. It was comforting to the families that only one man, someone who was extremely sensitive and knew them personally, someone with more than nineteen years at 40/35, was handling their calls. Kotula quickly developed a sense of how candid each person calling in wished him to be, and he tried, without ever being dishonest or offering too much hope, to bring as much humanity to the job as possible. Some family members called every half hour wanting updates. Was there anything new? Were there any voids? Did he think they might find voids?

106

Kotula felt himself pulled by the need of the families for hope, and, though he rationally knew better, he too began to believe that there might be a possibility of survival. Everything he said was tempered by the darkness he sensed descending on everyone, but he would not close off all hope. But hour by hour and then day by day, it got harder, like a battery that was getting weaker, and he could hear in the incoming calls, as Wednesday passed into Thursday and then Friday and Saturday, the flickering and dimming of all hope. In time, calls from wives were replaced by those from other relatives, as the wives wore down and became shakier. Finally, Sunday morning, Mike Kotula hung up the phone. He went to the bunk room, but he could not sleep, and so he headed over to P. D. O'Hurley's, a nearby pub that was a favorite of the men, and he had a few drinks. Only then could he sleep.

FIVE

Kevin Shea was found unconscious by Todd Maisel, a photographer from the New York *Daily News*, and some rescue workers. Some of what happened after the first collapse was related to him later by those who saved him. His own memory is fragile — he suffered a concussion and a broken neck among other severe injuries, and he was very lucky to be alive. Perhaps if Maisel had not found him, he might not have lived, and it was true that when Maisel first saw him lying there, covered with debris, he thought that Shea was dead.

Maisel, forty-one, had been up in Harlem on West 125th Street covering the New York mayoral primary that morning when the call had come in about the first plane. He rushed down to the World Trade Center to find a scene unlike any he had ever witnessed in his more than twelve years of photographing on the streets — a kind of hell on earth all around him. The first thing he saw were the jumpers — he looked around just as one landed on and killed a thirty-seven-year-old fireman from Engine 216 named Danny Suhr. Other firemen were trying to drag

Suhr's body back. Later, Suhr's wife, Nancy, said that she believed that he had saved several of his colleagues' lives by keeping them from entering the towers.

At that moment, feeling too close to the epicenter, Maisel started moving back, heading toward Liberty Street. But there was one photo he knew he wanted: The Saint Nicholas Greek Orthodox Church stood nearby and Maisel wanted to frame a shot with the cross of the church in the foreground and the smoking inferno of the south tower in the background. But even as he focused on the tower, it started to collapse. Maisel started running as fast as he could, hoping desperately to be fast enough to escape it.

He dove into the lobby of 90 West Street just as the tower collapsed. The exact time, it would be determined later, was 9:59 a.m. Then the ceiling and the walls of 90 West began to come down. The air was so thick with dust that it was almost impossible either to breathe or to see. Maisel was sure he was going to die if he stayed, so he started crawling backward — he could not go forward because there was a wall in front of him. What saved him and a number of others he aided in those most dangerous moments, he was later sure, was that he was carrying a bottle of water; thus he was able to drink and get the thick dust out of his throat and eyes. He shouted to the others in the room to follow his voice, and he tried as best he could to share his water with them.

Once outside, he snapped a few more pictures — he would later talk about a photojournalist's sacred obligation to record history — but soon he decided that this was a time when saving lives was more important than taking pictures. He helped get a couple of firemen to safety. *How odd,* he thought, *me rescuing the rescuers.* That was when he stumbled on Kevin Shea near the junction of Liberty and West streets. At first he thought Shea was dead, but then Maisel took his pulse and found feeble signs of life. Maisel, aware of his own fragile good fortune, was sure that Shea had been very close to the south tower, in an area where almost everyone else had been killed, and that he had been blown perhaps thirty or forty feet by the concussion from the collapse; then Shea must have crawled as many as 150 to 200 feet, to the place where Maisel eventually found him. No one who was not there, Maisel believed, could ever comprehend the power and sound of the explosion when the towers collapsed or could understand what a miracle it was that Shea survived.

Almost as soon as Maisel found Shea, Richie Nogan, a fireman who had gotten separated from his company, Ladder 113 of Brooklyn, during the collapse, stumbled over to help. Nogan had survived the fall of the south tower by hiding behind a car. Now he saw Maisel bending over a crumpled body and heard the photographer yell out that the man might still be alive, and that he was a fireman. Nogan rushed over. "I'm your brother," he said to the barely conscious Shea, using the phrase by which firemen refer to one another, "and I'll be with you until we can get you out of this." Nogan was amazed that Shea was alive, and sure that he had been thrown at least half a block by the implosion, in which cars had been tossed around as if they were children's toys.

Maisel and Nogan decided that Shea was in desperate shape, so they cut off some of his clothes. His body was all bruised, and he was moving in and out of consciousness. Nogan told Shea that it looked like he had lost a thumb. "That's okay. I've got another one," Shea answered. They thought it was extremely dangerous ministering to Shea where he was, that they might be hit by other collapses. The north tower had not yet come down, so Maisel and Nogan strapped Shea onto a backboard that Maisel found. Trying to protect Shea's head, they carried him to the corner of West Street and Albany. By then other men had arrived to help with the rescue. (Later one of the doctors who tended to Shea said the rescuers had done an amazingly good job; had they messed up with his head just slightly, Shea might have been paralyzed for life. Somehow, under these combat conditions, they had gotten it just right.) "Where are the others? Is everyone okay? Is everyone okay?" Shea kept asking, and one of the rescuers told him, "Yeah, sure, they're okay, they're out there laughing." Just then the rescuers heard another deep rumble and the explosion that was the north tower collapsing. The time was 10:28 a.m. Shea passed out again, only to become conscious long enough once more to ask if the other tower had collapsed.

Shea's rescuers needed to get him out of there. There was a car nearby, and they got Shea to it, but they couldn't close the door on the car with him lying on his board. They tracked down an ambulance, though, and the ambulance took them as far south as it could. Then they carried him to the Hudson River and lowered him into a police boat. Thus Shea became one of the first firemen ferried over to Jersey City, where a triage center had already been set up. His injuries, however, were so serious that he was quickly taken to the hospital.

Joviana Perez-Mercado was at her job handling insurance claims at a hospital in the Bronx that morning when she heard that a plane had crashed into the World Trade Center. She called her husband, Steve, who was not supposed to be working at the firehouse that morning, but who had rearranged his schedule in order to take care of some family chores later in the week. "Is there a fire at the World Trade Center?" she asked him. There was a printer at the firehouse that ticked off all the local fire news, and there was nothing on it about a fire, just a report of a plane hitting one of the towers. "Is that all?" she asked.

Yes, he said. But a few minutes later, when the second plane hit, she called him back. "I know, honey," he said. "Look, I've got to go. I can't talk any longer. I'll talk to you later." And that was it, she thought later, that was it.

At the firehouse Steve Mercado was sometimes called Steve Muchacho, but more often Rico, a nickname coined by his close friend Mike Kotula, after "Rico Suave," the early-'90s hit by the pop singer Gerardo. Mercado had grown up in the Castle Hill section of the Bronx. His father, who was Puerto Rican, worked for the government handling unemployment cases, and his mother, who was half Irish and half German, worked for the school system. By dint of his last name, however, Mercado was, according to firehouse ethnicity, simply Spanish.

Mercado was the resident mimic, and he was a brilliant one, so good, the other men thought, that he could be a professional comedian. He would sit quietly watching the other firemen, studying their idiosyncrasies, their manners, body language, and speech patterns, and then when the time was right, he would do a wonderful impersonation of them. He was generally careful never to push it too far, to stay on the gentler side of the line that separated humor from cruelty. But if you were sitting around in the kitchen, having a cup of coffee, and Steve Mercado was there as well, studying you a little too closely, it was time to get up and move away, because he was almost surely working on his repertoire. He also liked to study the newspapers every morning, clipping headlines ("New Treatment for Bowel Problems," "Turns Down $10 Million One-Season Contract, Feels He's Worth More") to attach to an appropriate photo among those of all the men, which hung upstairs in the house.

The role of the mimic was important to him long before he went to the firehouse, Joviana thought, but it was there that his talent had flowered. Some of it was done, she believed, partly in self-defense, because he was ethnically the new boy, being half Puerto Rican. If he was zinging the others, then it was a sign he was one of the boys; also, if he was zinging them, then they would be just a little more on the defensive and perhaps reluctant to zing him. Ironically, he did not even speak Spanish, much to the irritation of some of his officers. When he was growing up, his family had spoken English in the home. Sometimes when the firemen would go into a building where no one spoke English, one of the officers would summon Mercado to be the translator, a role at which he always failed miserably.

The longer he was at the firehouse, though, and the more accepted he became there, Joviana thought, the more it seemed to stir his ethnic pride. He now wanted his own sons, Skylar, six, and Austin, two, to speak Spanish. That became something of a bone of contention in their home. Joviana, who was Puerto Rican and who spoke

Spanish fluently, would tell him that if the boys spoke Spanish, he would not understand them. "You'll be left out, and you won't like it," she said. Still, he lobbied for Spanish, and if Jovi's mother spoke English to the boys, he would get upset. There was no doubt that he was becoming prouder of his own Hispanic heritage. When it was his turn to cook, he would ask his mother-in-law for her recipes, and when it came time for the firehouse picnic, he would work with her to make her Spanish-style roast pork, which was considered something of a specialty. Invariably it was one of the first things that disappeared from the picnic table.

Living in the city had become ever more important to Mercado. He had grown up there, and he had played stickball there as a boy. Now he wanted his sons to play the game, and he had even written a poem about stickball, "Our Game," in which he explained how the sport had brought him and his father closer together. He was president of the New York Emperors Stickball League, and he was constantly campaigning for stickball to become an official Olympic sport. If that did not seem likely to most of the other men in the firehouse, he did not care. He was certain that the International Olympic Committee would eventually recognize it, probably by 2016, at which time Skylar would be coming of age as a world-class stickball prospect. For that reason he was reluctant to leave the city for the suburbs, even as his family expanded and they needed more room, because in the suburbs, they didn't play stickball. If they left the city, the Olympic dream for Skylar and Austin would die, so he looked hard for affordable housing in the city, and finally found what was for him an ideal place in the Bronx.

Ray Pfeifer loved the shameless way that Mercado would do *anything* to promote stickball — and himself. No one at the firehouse, Pfeifer thought, worked harder than Mercado, and no one had more fun. "I don't think I ever knew anyone who enjoyed the firehouse so much, and who took so much pleasure in just being there every day with the other guys," Pfeifer recalled of his friend. The two liked to cook together, and they were both exceptionally proud of the moment a few years earlier when they had won the Food Network's firehouse chili cooking contest with their "White Heat" turkey chili, featuring Mercado's not-so-secret ingredient: dried jalapeños that he had stored for a full year.

Mercado and Pfeifer's was a most unlikely friendship. Mercado was part Puerto Rican from the Bronx, and Pfeifer was German and unabashedly suburban, from Levittown, Long Island, a place where people had moved after World War II in order to avoid, among other things, the Hispanic migration to the city. They would constantly inflict ethnic zingers on each other — jokes that would never be permitted by outsiders. Indeed, if anyone from the outside had said such things, there surely would have been a brawl, with all the firefighters on the side of their own man. Thus Pfeifer would call Mercado "a stupid spic," and Mercado, in turn, would say that Pfeifer was not just from Levittown, but from "lily-white Levittown," and that he would never dare to visit Mercado in the South Bronx, because he was too white to find his way around there.

If Mercado seemed edgy on the surface, always ready to zing someone else, he was also, the others thought, unusually sensitive. One of the things he loved about being a fireman, Jovi thought, was the respect that he and the other men got when they drove to and from a fire — the people in the streets waving and smiling at them, and even occasionally, cheering. The respect that went with the job, he told Jovi, was one of the things he liked best about what he did — people understood that what he did mattered. About six years earlier, on West Seventy-fourth Street, there had been a very tough fire, from which the men had pulled several people, including a young woman who seemed in very bad shape. Mercado had performed CPR on her, and she seemed to be improving. They took her to the hospital. The word was that she was going to recover. The next morning, after Mercado got up, he went directly to the hospital, only to discover that she had died during the night. He was, the other men realized when he got to work, utterly disconsolate.

Back in Islip, Long Island, Marion Otten finally heard from family members that her brother Michael had made it out safely. That meant her thoughts were now only about her husband, her Michael. She knew that it was her part of the bargain of being married to a fireman that she was not to worry about her husband. The job, her husband always insisted, was not that dangerous. When she would raise the question of danger, her Michael would talk about his own father, Richard Otten, who had been a fireman. "Look at him," Michael Otten would say. "Thirty years on the job before he retired, and he got maybe a couple of bruises and bumps, but nothing ever happened — or nothing serious anyway." So, nothing bad was going to happen to him. His and Marion's matter-of-fact conversations about his work had practically become ritualized: "How was work?" "Good." "What kind of runs did you go on?" "The usual." "What kind of usual?" "Gas leaks. A car fire. The usual stuff. Nothing very much." Nothing very much, she thought, except sometimes she knew, nothing very much meant that he and the other men had risked their lives.

Some days when he would tell her that it had all been just the usual, his father would call, and Michael would talk with him about the jobs he had been on, fireman to fireman. She would listen in, feeling, as so many of the wives did at such moments, like something of an outsider as

118

they talked shop. Michael would go into considerable detail — who had been good, and who had not been good. By overhearing those conversations, she realized that it was never routine. But she also knew that it was part of the code of the men that they did not want their wives to worry, so they deliberately edited the information they gave them. That created a special dilemma for the wives, she thought: They had to pretend that the constant possibility of danger did not exist, when in fact they all knew that it *did*. "The job," she said, "is to learn how to live around it — you pretend that it's not really there, and that your lives are as normal as everyone else's."

In October he would have marked sixteen years with the department, and they were happy years for them as a couple. The tragedy occurred, his family and friends thought, at the very best moment of his life; he had a wonderful family, he was immensely popular with the other men at his firehouse, and he loved his job. Her Michael was a marvelous, exuberant, playful husband, Marion Otten thought. She loved the contradictions in him, that this man who did dangerous things was always playing with his sons or cooking. In fact, he loved to cook. He also loved to shop for food — they would argue over whose turn it was both to cook and to shop. He spent more time watching the Food Network than most women she knew. One other thing that set him apart from almost everyone else, she recalled, was that he was always smiling; later, after it was all over and she had accepted the idea of his death, she looked through their family photo album. She was astonished to see that Michael was smiling in every single snapshot in the book.

He was a fireman's son and a fireman's grandson, and according to everyone's memories of him, he had loved to try on his father's uniform as a boy. Henry Otten, his grandfather, had been a fireman in Brooklyn and Queens, and Henry's son Richard had often hung out at the firehouse when he was a kid, and had sometimes even shown up at the fires the men were covering. In time, Richard Otten became a fireman, and he had enjoyed taking his son Michael, the second of his five children, to the firehouse — especially on Thursdays every other week, when they went in to pick up Richard's paycheck. Starting when Michael was about five years old, that had become a family ritual, and there would often be other kids there. The men always made a fuss over the kids and let them play on the rigs. When Michael was twelve, he began to hang out a bit more, at Ladder 24, near Madison Square Garden, and he would even sleep over once in a while, and slide down the pole with the men when there was an alarm. Sometimes he would put on some turnout gear — well, not exactly a complete set of turnout gear, and perhaps it was a little large for him — and he would even go off on some runs with the men. Richard Otten thought his son had never really considered anything else as a career.

Marion Otten agreed. It was, she thought, the only thing he had ever thought seriously of doing. When he got out of high school, he bounced around a bit, going from job to job, making just enough money to be able to have a good time. He briefly went to college, but it was obvious that his mind and heart were elsewhere, and there had been no great effort on the part of the college officials to dissuade him from leaving. Michael was still kicking around somewhat aimlessly when he met Marion Otten, who was no kin, and who was already quite serious about her purpose in life. She was the daughter of German immigrants who had come to the United States in the 1950s. Hardworking and pragmatic, they intended that their children would focus their energies in order to succeed in this new country — nothing would be wasted. When Marion met Michael, he was twenty-three and she was twenty, and she was studying to become an occupational therapist. She did not seem like a person who was going to spend much time with a man who wanted to coast through life.

At the time Michael was still hanging out, making just enough money to party, but, Marion suspected, he was already beginning to work out the puzzle of his life, and was aware that the time was drawing near when he had to make some hard choices. She had already completed two years toward her degree at Stony Brook, and was transferring to a Brooklyn medical school to finish. Michael was working for Northrop Grumman out on Long Island, but not taking the job very seriously. Eventually he was let go, which came as a genuine surprise to him. It was the one time she had seen him unhappy — it wasn't that he really liked the job, but he was still shocked at being fired.

He had taken the fire department test for the first time when he was eighteen and had not done well. Having been as casual about it as he was about the other things in his life, he had not prepared very seriously, but rather just showed up that day. That he had done so poorly, Marion thought, was something of a disappointment to his father. But now, having met Marion and beginning to take a hard look at his life and the options left to him, Michael Otten started getting more serious. Eventually he studied hard and took special classes to prepare for the firemen's exam, and he got himself in very good shape. He nailed it, getting a 100 on the written part, and a ninety-five on the physical.

It was the right life for him; as his friend Mike Kotula would say after his death, "Mikey, with that lovely smile, made it more fun for everyone. Everyone else wanted to smile as well." At the house, he was known as the expert on classic comedies: He knew every line from *The Three Stooges*; he could do a very respectable Jackie Gleason on *The Honeymooners*, getting the lines out before Gleason spoke them; and he was, the others thought, just about up to speed memorizing *Seinfeld* routines.

Like his sitcoms, Otten took his ancestral pride very seriously. He was German in a predominantly Irish environment. Because of this ethnic tilt, he had to scramble for his turf, and when Pfeifer showed up for his first day, they bonded with each other practically from the moment they met. Otten came up to him and asked, "What's your last name?" "Pfeifer," he answered. "That's a German name, right?" Otten asked. Pfeifer said it was. "Are there any other Germans here?" Pfeifer asked. "No, just the two of us," Otten said. So Otten got Pfeifer a locker next to his own, and that area immediately became known as Kraut Korner, decorated with various German flags and decals. (When a phone call would come in for either of them, and Bruce Gary answered, he would yell out, "Will one of the two Nazis pick up the phone?") Otten would refrain from marching in the St. Patrick's Day Parade, although many of the non-Irish firemen did so as a point of solidarity with their Irish colleagues. Otten marched in the German-American Steuben Parade instead. And each year for Oktoberfest he would host a party with beer and bratwurst at his house — the men called it the Ottenfest.

Otten and Pfeifer became even closer when Caryn Pfeifer, Ray's wife, was facing a serious kidney operation, for which her sister was going to be the kidney donor. The only area hospital where they could get two surgery rooms side-by-side was at Boston's Beth Israel, so Ray had to go up to Boston during that period, often sleeping in the car to save on hotel costs, until friends made a connection with a Boston firehouse, Ladder 4, where he could stay overnight. In those difficult months, it was Mikey Otten who helped him, who would drive to Boston with him, and who would stay on the phone for long hours with him, to reassure him that he wasn't alone, that it would all turn out okay. It was the kind of thing family did, thought Pfeifer, and in the firehouse, your friends became like an extension of your family.

Over the summer Otten had been studying hard for the lieutenant's exam. The first time he had taken it, he had not prepared sufficiently, much as with his first attempt to get into the department. "I got a seventy-one," he told Pfeifer, and Pfeifer was pleased. That was pretty good for the first time on such a tough test, Pfeifer thought, and he praised Otten for doing so well. "Yeah," said Otten, "seventy-one wrong." But he planned to take it again in October, and this time Otten had worked hard to prepare and had told his father that he was very confident about passing.

Kevin Bracken tended to be more than a little overweight, and his nickname was Pugsley, after the character on *The Addams Family* — they even put it on the back of his softball uniform. That morning his wife, Jennifer Liang, was with a neighbor, and they had turned on the television set just as the second plane hit. Jennifer immediately called the firehouse and was told that the truck had just left. At first she, like many others, thought they had probably left too late for the worst of it.

In those early hours, she did not worry much about her husband. At one point she thought she saw Ladder 35 on television, but it was hard to know for sure. Eventually, as morning turned into afternoon, she began to call the firehouse hourly, but she still was not that worried. The absence of calls from Kevin was not unusual because he was in no way the kind of man who felt that he had to check in with his wife all the time. By mid-afternoon, though, she did begin to worry, and at around 4 p.m. she went over to the firehouse and ended up staying there through the night and the following day.

Some of the other wives had come as well, and everyone there was trying to hold out hope for the men. But very early on, Jennifer had an eerie feeling that they were all gone. All of them. It was the absence of any news — not just from Kevin, but from all of them. All those talented, tough, resilient men, and not a single word from or about any of them. As it grew darker, she had a hard time watching the men from other shifts return from their search-and-rescue missions. Pain and exhaustion were all over their faces, and they could barely look at her and the other wives. She was scared for them, worried that they were going to push themselves too hard. If that happened, even more men were going to get killed, and they had lost enough men already, she thought. There was a brief flurry of hope sometime on Wednesday when the news circulated that Kevin Shea had been found and taken to a hospital. There was talk that this was just the beginning and that they were going to find others, but she had her doubts. Some of the officers were trying to rally everyone's spirits: *We're going to find them, we know they're out there. It's just a matter of time.* But Jennifer did not think time was an ally.

If there was any redeeming aspect about what had happened, she later decided, it was that she and Kevin had had no unresolved issues between them. They had loved each other completely from the start, and they had always understood how lucky they were. There was nothing she wished she had said to him before he died. In late August they had finished the last major stage of renovating their apartment, just five blocks from the firehouse — they had taken two small apartments and merged them into one by knocking down some walls. Kevin, aided by his father, Hugh, a retired army sergeant major, and some of the other men from the firehouse, had just put in an oak floor, and though there were still a good many smaller jobs to be done, the couple had been able to move their furniture back in. After a year in which the apartment seemed semi-habitable at best, Kevin had been able to spend a few days there, sitting on his own couch, watching his own television. During the renovation Hugh Bracken had come down from Cape Cod for a week each month to assist his son, and Jennifer had been moved by the sheer sweetness of father and son working together in such total harmony — both of them skilled carpenters, both of them enjoying not just their work, but working together. Hugh Bracken was particularly pleased that his son had become an even finer craftsman than he was.

Jennifer had never worried very much about the dangers inherent in being a fireman because Kevin had told her never to worry. There was, after all, the famous Bracken Bounce, which was proof of the constancy of his good luck. The term was coined by a friend who played golf with him on a day when Kevin had hit a drive that was heading far into the woods, only to strike a tree and bounce back right smack onto the middle of the fairway. The Bracken Bounce, the friend had called it, and the term stuck. He might not be a great golfer, but in golf as in life, Kevin did better because of the Bracken Bounce. Good things always happened to him, his friends thought — just look at him finding a wonderful young woman such as Jennifer. Bright, pretty, and hip, she had graduated with exceptional grades from Mount Holyoke, the famed elite Seven Sisters college in western Massachusetts, and had gotten her MBA at NYU. She might have married someone who had graduated from Harvard or Columbia or Princeton, a doctor, lawyer, or stockbroker; instead she had fallen completely in love with Kevin, whose academic record was a bit spotty, and for whom college had never really been in the picture. His previous jobs, before becoming a fireman, had been as a salesman for the American Bartenders School and working regional exhibitions for the rice pudding industry.

Guys like Kevin, his friends had teased, had no right to find someone as lovely as Jennifer. She was second-generation Chinese American, and she thought Kevin was the most optimistic person she had ever met. Always upbeat, always sunny. Some of her old friends had seen the gap in their backgrounds and wondered whether the two of them had much in common, but she loved the fact that he was smart in a way that was tuned to the real world. He could fix anything, for instance. She was tired of bright young men who were full of themselves, but who could not repair anything and were condescending toward those who could. Jennifer and Kevin, Ray Pfeifer said not long after the September tragedy, it was hard to think of them not being together, because they were so good together that it was like they were one person.

They had been together for eleven years, and married for five. They had met on the train platform at Central Islip, where they both lived back in 1990, when Kevin was twenty-six and Jennifer was twenty-one. "You missed your train," he said to her one morning, while she was waiting, and he was right. She asked him how he knew. "I've seen you on the other train quite often," he said, but she was sure there was more to it, that because she was so noisy on the train, talking with her friends, that he had taken note of her. If anything had tested their marriage, it was the year and a half of living among the detritus and upheaval of renovation, while doing most of the work themselves. Even so, there had been relatively little tension between them, mostly, she decided, because his disposition was so positive. Perhaps, Jennifer Liang thought, birth order was responsible — he was the youngest of five children, with three older sisters, and he had always felt immensely loved. Whatever the reason, he had come out amazingly centered and comfortable with himself.

His sisters agreed. He was *always* happy and had been since he was a little boy. Rules that had applied to his older siblings seemed not to apply to him, because he tended simply to disregard any rules he seriously disliked. Kevin never fought life — instead he always turned it to his advantage. He was, not surprisingly, the favorite uncle at family gatherings. When the children of his sister Mary Bracken Carlson were young, Uncle Kevin had wired a walkie-talkie into the Christmas tree, so that the Christmas tree would talk to the kids. Remarkably, the tree seemed to know not only their names, but a good deal about them as well. Later, because his name looked so similar to that of his niece, Kerin, on the cards attached to the Christmas presents, Kevin would open at least one of her gifts each year and pretend it was for him; once, when she was about twelve, he had opened a present containing a nightgown and he had put it on and worn it for a few hours.

Kevin had a tendency to play down the dangers of any fire he had been on, even when he was talking with the other men. He might come back to the house, and someone would ask, "How was it, Kevin?" And he would answer, "It was hot, it was smoky, and we put it out." He tried to make it all seem like just another day at the office, even if his office was a bit hotter and smokier. "Was it scary, Kevin?" Jennifer would ask him when he came home from a fire, and he would always answer, "No, no, no, of course it wasn't scary."

Besides, he was always calm. Early on in their relationship, she was amazed by the constancy of his calm. "Doesn't anything throw you?" she would ask, and he would shrug his shoulders. Everything was always going to work out and it was always going to work out for the best, he would say. And so, she was not to worry, and she didn't. Perhaps, she later mused, if they had had children, they might have worried, but they were still young. They had always thought they had lots of time.

SIX

Michael Lynch and Stephanie Luccioni were engaged to be married on November 16 at St. Benedict's Parish in the Bronx, and at around 10:30 on the night before the tragedy, they talked to each other on the phone about the wedding. He was a probie at the firehouse, on rotation from Ladder 32 in the Bronx, and had been with the 40/35 men for only a few months. Stephanie was at home, addressing their wedding invitations on her computer and feeling that she was falling behind on the enormous amount of work still to be done to prepare for the wedding. "Oh my God, I'm way behind in this," she had told Michael, who was working a twenty-four-hour shift at the firehouse. "Don't worry about it," he said. "It'll work out. Everything's going to be fine." The remark reminded her that she was the organized one, who wanted everything done exactly on time, and he was the casual one, who was sure things would always sort themselves out. "Well, do you still want to marry me?" she asked, teasing him. "Of course I do," he answered, "and the invitations will get done, and we'll have a wonderful wedding."

He would be thirty-one in December, and Stephanie was thirty. They had met because she had been a pal of his younger sister, Colleen, and as a teenager had hung out at his house. The Lynches were a large, joyous family; Michael was the seventh child of ten and the fifth son. Their house seemed to be open for everyone, filled all the time with the Lynch children, and the friends of the Lynch children, and the friends of the friends of the Lynch children. Thus it was not that unusual for one of the Lynch boys to become interested in the friend of one of the Lynch daughters. In the case of Stephanie, she was there so often, having been pulled in by the warmth of the family, that Colleen liked to refer to her as the eleventh Lynch child. In particular Stephanie loved the Christmastime brunches served after morning Mass on December 24, when Jack Lynch would cook an immense feast for everyone, and there would be thirty or forty people there. That was the kind of home that she hoped to have for her family one day, albeit perhaps with fewer children.

In August, Michael had been the best man at his brother Thomas's wedding. Michael was two years older than Thomas, and the two were unusually close, more like twins, Jack Lynch, their father, thought. It was almost as if they had their own special language that excluded all others. When, as part of his best-man responsibilities, Michael toasted Thomas, the toast was exceptionally graceful, his siblings recalled, at once loving, funny, and eloquent; Thomas, he predicted, would live a rich, happy life, just as their parents had, and like them, he would have ten children. Jack Lynch had been impressed by how much his son had grown and matured, an impression shared by John Lynch, the eldest child in the family, some ten years older than Michael. After the wedding, John, who worked in London and had not seen much of his younger brother in recent years, took his father aside and said, "My God, he's turned into an absolutely wonderful young man. I'm really impressed — his confidence is amazing."

Each summer the Lynches would take a family vacation on the Jersey Shore, gathering as a clan of some thirty people from three generations for two weeks or so. In 2001, for the first time, Michael and Stephanie had come as a couple. Jack Lynch had watched the two of them together and had seen that confidence and happiness in his son, and he had been thrilled. Jack believed that his son now had the two things he had always wanted: the job he had always sought and a girl he loved and wanted to marry. Michael had at this moment, his father believed, everything in the world to look forward to.

Both Jack and his wife, Kathleen Lynch, were born in Ireland, he in County Kerry, she in County Sligo. He had come to America when he was twenty-one, and had worked for thirty-three years for the New York City Transit Authority, running the organization's garage in East New

York as his last job. He and Kathleen had always lived in the Bronx, first in the Fordham Road area, and then in the Throg's Neck section, staying in the latter neighborhood for some thirty-five years, even as it became a little less Irish and a little more diverse. The couple had not actually set out to have so large a family, but it had happened, and they always managed. He had his salary from the Transit Authority and moonlighted as a plumber; she ran the family finances with great skill and determination, and if she expected that the bills for the month might be a little higher than usual, say, because of some extra medical or clothing expenses, she would tell him how much she thought she needed, and he would make it his assignment to earn the extra money. Somehow he always managed to do it.

Of their ten children, eight went to college, and all of them could have. Michael went to Iona, a Catholic college in nearby Westchester, but he did not want to be a professional. He had always wanted to be a fireman. That was his dream as a boy, and it never changed. For a time after college, he worked in the training program of Dean Witter, a financial company that was housed at the time, ironically enough, in Building Five of the World Trade Center. He did quite well there by all accounts, for he was smart, attractive, courteous, and hardworking. His father thought it might turn out to be a very good career for him — working at a prestigious financial house with so much opportunity; eventually, he thought, Michael might do very well there as a stockbroker, becoming a good deal more affluent than he himself had been. "It's a very good place and a very good company," he told his son, "and I think you can do well there." "But that's not what I want to do," Michael replied. "I don't want to be a stockbroker." "Well, you at least ought to think about it," Jack Lynch insisted, anxious that his son not walk away too quickly from a life that might be both easier and more materially rewarding, and in which he might be able to use his many talents. "Dad, I don't have to give it a second thought — it's not what I want. I really know that. Dad, I *know* what I want," Michael said, and that was that.

That he was not interested in Dean Witter did not surprise Stephanie; she knew Michael hated working indoors, sitting in front of a computer. When he was at Dean Witter, he had seemed bored with life, so lethargic after work that he had had little interest in their doing anything together in the evening. By contrast, when he became a fireman, he never seemed more alive, and his exuberance from the job carried over into his social life.

Theirs was not a firefighting family. But Michael had always been drawn to the profession. As a boy, he had been fascinated by fire trucks. "When kids are young, they all want to be firemen," said his brother Tom. "Most of us change, but Michael wanted it as a boy, and he

135

wanted it as a man. In fact, he never wanted anything else." For Michael it had always been a romantic calling, his family thought. In addition, his father believed, he was drawn to it because he possessed a certain selflessness; Michael was perhaps the most sensitive of his children, the unofficial peacemaker in the family, recalled Jack Lynch. He had chosen to be a fireman because he had always seen himself in the role of helping others. "It was always a calling with him," Jack said later, "it was not just a job."

Jack Lynch did not usually listen to the radio during breakfast, but on the morning of September 11, he had turned it on. When the first bulletin about the first plane came in, he and Kathleen immediately switched on the television. At first, he thought of the many friends of the family who worked in that building, and he speculated rather casually to his wife that Michael would probably be going down there. As they continued to watch, the second plane hit. Suddenly it was all beyond his comprehension: "Something I could not get my mind around," he remembered. "It was like watching a science fiction movie at home, except that it was live, and it was real, and it was not going to go away."

Then he and Kathleen began the long, cruel wait for a phone call from Michael, because they knew he would call if he could. At first they decided he was too busy but as the day wore on, they became more nervous. When friends called, they would ask them, as politely as possible, to get off the phone because they wanted to keep the line open for their son. Michael had a cell phone, and they called it; it rang but there was no answer. At first they thought this was a sign that he was all right, but then they began to realize it simply meant that he had probably left the phone in his locker back at the firehouse.

Stephanie, who was a guidance counselor at Christ the King High School, was at work in Queens that morning. She and Michael had not talked in the morning because, as usual, she had to be out of the house by 6:00 a.m. in order to make the commute from the Bronx to Queens. As news of the attack spread throughout the school — and it was a terrible morning there because many of the students had parents who worked in the World Trade Center — she had, like several of the other friends and family members of the 40/35 men, taken solace in the fact that the firehouse was so far uptown that Michael would be safe. She was let out of school early and drove home, getting stuck for six hours on the Van Wyck Expressway. Without her cell phone that day, she was unable to talk to anyone, but, in her stopped car, she had a clear view of the World Trade Center site, shrouded in heavy, black smoke.

Gradually the reality dawned on the Lynches that they had lost Michael. Two days after the attack, Jack visited the site with an old friend of his named Mike Dolan, a senior project manager for Turner Construction in Chicago, who had

137

flown in when he learned that Michael had been at Ground Zero and was missing. The two old friends walked down Liberty Street, which ran along the south side of the south tower, and then they walked past the wreckage of Ladder 10, getting as close to Ground Zero as they could. At one point Dolan, who was a few feet ahead of Jack Lynch, stopped and looked at the sight of the awful destruction and then, with tears in his eyes, he turned back to his friend, and said that even in his wildest thoughts he couldn't imagine anyone surviving; with his engineering background, he understood the totality of the pancake collapse of the two buildings and the unbelievable tonnage that had fallen straight down on itself. The chance of anyone surviving it, he said, did not exist. That night, Jack told Kathleen what Michael Dolan had said.

But Jack Lynch could not bring himself to tell Stephanie. He waited a week, not wanting to cast any additional shadow on her, knowing that in the greater optimism and innocence of youth, she still believed that somehow Michael would survive. Finally, when it was clear she had given up all hope, she turned to the man who would have been her father-in-law, and who now loved her as if she was one of his daughters. "What people don't understand," she told him, "is that no one ever loved anyone like Michael and I loved each other."

Michael Roberts was the quiet one. Sean

Newman, who had worked with him at Engine 224 in Brooklyn Heights, thought that the thirty-year-old Roberts had been more at home there because it was smaller, housing only one rig, and that the sheer size of 40/35 somehow had made him quieter. Certainly it was true that the larger the group hanging around the kitchen table, the quieter he became; he only opened up with a very small group. Roberts seemed more than most firemen to live within himself, somewhat apart from the noise and bawdiness of the house. There was, Newman thought, an intensity to him underneath that quiet surface — he was very competitive when he played sports, and, as a fireman, he would become quite frustrated when he thought the rig did not get out of the firehouse fast enough. He hated the idea that another company might get to the scene of a fire faster than his own.

For Roberts, as for so many of the others, being a fireman was a family thing. His father, Tom Roberts, was a retired captain, and a number of Tom's cousins were also firemen. He thought that his son Michael's earliest memories were of firehouse picnics, of being among all these men who felt so warmly toward his father and himself. When Michael was a year old, one of his first presents had been a navy-blue outfit with a fire truck on it, and his mother had embroidered above the truck the words *Dad and Me.*

Tom Roberts had always thought his was a

wonderful life, much better, for example, than the lives of cops in terms of the kind of treatment and respect he got within the neighborhoods he served. The cops, he thought, no matter how well they protected people, almost always generated resentment, whereas firemen, with the exception of a few bad moments, were generally viewed benignly. This affected how you thought about yourself and your job. Besides, when a fireman put out a fire, it stayed out; whereas when the cops arrested a hoodlum, he was, more often than not, it seemed, back on the streets in a few days.

Michael, from the time he was a little boy had always been both shy and quiet. Part of the reason had been his struggle with vision when he was young. He wore glasses and he had had a lazy eye, for which he had to do years of exercises in order to strengthen it. That had helped him when he took the firemen's test, because as a result of the exercises, his vision and reflexes were very good, and it helped him later in firehouse Ping-Pong games; he was rarely beaten, and, with his long reach, he was known at the Brooklyn Heights house as The Condor.

Tom and his wife, Paulette, had encouraged Michael to go to college, wanting him to aim for more than they had had, but he had been reluctant. He started out at Rockland Community College and after two years went on to the University at Buffalo, where he studied a variety of different subjects, none of which greatly interested him. Tom pushed him toward becoming a social worker and Paulette toward psychology, but he had no interest in either career. "You try and give them the advantages you never had," Tom Roberts said, "and what they want is the life you had. When I was young, we did it because we had no alternative, no other possibilities. But that was a much poorer country, and most of us who chose the fire department had less opportunity — we were not going to go to college, it was just not in the cards. But now we watch our children grow up in far better circumstances than we did, and we encourage them to go to college the way Michael did, so they will have more choices. And they do that, dutifully, they go off to college and they give it a try, and then, when they finish, they go into the department because they have watched us, and ours is the life they want."

When Michael Roberts started going through the process of preparing himself for the firemen's test, his somewhat uneasy father questioned him. "Are you sure this is what you really want?" he asked. "After all, you've got a college education." Yes, Michael replied, he was sure this was what he wanted. "Why?" his father asked. "Because you always came home from work happy," his son answered.

Tom Roberts was quietly pleased when his son went into the department; now they could talk shop, critiquing fires and the performances of men from different units. It was odd, Tom

141

thought, but when he had been a fireman, he had never worried much about his own safety. Now, however, he worried about his son. For the first time, he had a sense of what it must be like to be the spouse of a fireman. The Astoria Father's Day fire, in which the three men had died, had shaken him.

Teresa Ivey and Michael met at a barbecue on Labor Day in the summer of 1999. She was twenty-five at the time, and that summer, thinking of prospective boyfriends, she had decided it might be nice to date a fireman because what they did each day was so valuable. At the barbecue she had noticed a tall, attractive young man standing off to the side. She asked him what he did, and he said he was a fireman, and she said something to the effect of how admirable that was. This surprised him, and he asked her, "You'd be willing to date someone knowing that each time he went off to work he might not come back at night because of the danger?" "Yes," she answered, "because if something terrible happened, I'd be able to say that the person I loved died doing something for other people." He called her for a date almost immediately afterward, and they had been together ever since.

Teresa thought he was the gentlest kind of man, soft-spoken, and, above all, selfless. That last quality, she was sure, was why he had become a fireman. If you had met Michael at a party, she thought, you might well have gotten his profession wrong. What she especially loved about him was that his belief in her career matched her belief in his. She was a schoolteacher, with one master's degree, in English, and he was pushing her to go for a second one, in administration, because he was absolutely sure she would be a brilliant principal. If she was ever overloaded and pressed for time, he would help her grade papers. And he would not hesitate to shift his schedule to be with her and her eighth-grade students on a field trip or at a musical program at school.

They had been dating for two years, and two days before the tragedy she had teased him about when he was actually going to propose. "You'll know when I ask," he answered, laughing. She wanted a specific date, and he wanted a little more mystery. But she knew they would be engaged sometime in the middle of 2002, and she knew as well they were rock solid as a couple. Early in this relationship, she had, as in past ones, started to build an emotional wall around herself, to protect herself from any serious commitment. But he would have none of it. "You can try to leave, but you're not going anywhere," he told her. "I'm meant to be with you, and you're meant to be with me. So forget about getting out of it." He had been right, she decided.

Teresa was teaching at the Suffern, New York, middle school on the morning of September 11, and she was pulled out of class at exactly 8:59 a.m., thirteen minutes after the first crash. Her bosses knew that her father worked for the Port Authority in the south tower, and her sister worked in the Bankers Trust building just across the street.

Teresa called Michael at work, but he had already left on the truck, so she got him on his cell phone. "Oh my God," she said, "my father's there, and my sister's there." "I know," he said, "Kenny's there too." Kenny was Michael's younger brother, who had taken the written exam to become a fireman and who at the time was working for the Securities and Exchange Commission on the twelfth floor of Building Seven. Teresa knew Michael was going into a terrible situation. Her last words to him were: "Whatever you do, keep in touch! Keep in touch! Keep in touch!" He had promised he would, and then she said one more time, "Keep in touch!"

Her father and sister got out safely, as did Kenny. Later, Kenny discovered that Michael had called him at work after he, along with most of his friends, had left. Much later he heard on the phone message system the voice of a concerned older brother he would never see again.

Thomas and Paulette Roberts did not learn about the attack until relatively late on Tuesday. They had been driving to Hilton Head, South Carolina, for a vacation, and they had spent the night in a motel in North Carolina. They had breakfast early, before the first plane hit, and then got back on the road. Their daughter Lisa had given them a bunch of CDs, so they were not listening to the radio. They were anxious to make good time, and they did not stop for lunch until about 1:00 p.m. At the restaurant, Paulette overheard some people talking about a plane crash, but she had been unable to pick up on it. After lunch they pulled into a gas station, and for the first time they found out that two planes had hit the World Trade Center towers. With that, they drove on to Hilton Head as fast as possible, while trying unsuccessfully to place phone calls home from the occasional phone booths along the highway.

Upon their arrival around 4:00 p.m., they turned on the television and for the first time they understood the totality of the tragedy. They struggled to get through to their family in New York, because it was still extremely difficult to make phone connections to the city. At first they were more worried about Kenny than about Michael. They finally reached a neighbor, whom they told to break into their house because there might be a message on their answering machine, and they had forgotten the procedure needed to pick up messages from the road. But there were no messages from their kids. While they were on the phone, a call came in from Lisa, and a message was taken by the clerk at the front desk saying that Lisa and Kenny were all right, but that Michael was working and that no one had heard from him.

Tom and Paulette were exhausted, and they

briefly debated whether or not to spend the night in South Carolina before heading back to New York. In the end, they decided, exhausted or not, to return because they knew they weren't going to get any sleep that night if they stayed in the motel. Taking turns as drivers and napping along the side of the road, they finally arrived home around 3:00 p.m. on Wednesday, Kenny and Lisa were there, but there was still no word from Michael. They immediately feared the worst.

Vincent Morello was the son of a fireman, brother of a fireman, cousin and nephew of firemen. He, however, had never intended to be a fireman. His father, John Morello, who had reached the rank of battalion chief in Manhattan, never pushed the job with him, and when Vincent finished high school, his only interest seemed to be working as a mechanic at a local gas station. The Morellos wanted more for their son than a career in a gas station, though, and encouraged Vincent to try college — at least, John argued, go to college and take some business courses, so you can one day own your own garage — but it had not interested Vincent. After only one year at St. John's University, in Queens, he was back at his first love: the garage, where he was so innately gifted with tools. When John suggested that Vincent think of becoming a fireman and take the exam — just as a fall-back position — Vincent merely laughed and placed a hand on each of his father's shoulders. "Dad, when a building is on fire," he said, "the smart people are the ones running to get out."

If anything, that answer had seemed to please John Morello. He was sure that he had never pushed either of his sons to follow him into the department. Actually, he was sure he had discouraged them — in part, he later said, because he wanted them to have something more than he did, and in part because he knew, as only an experienced fireman could know, just how dangerous the job could be. There had been a moment in 1980 when, as a captain at Ladder 161 in Coney Island, he was sure that he was going to die. There was a fire in a restaurant on the ground floor of a building, and he and two men from his house had gone up to the second floor, looking for survivors. As the fire got worse and worse, he sent the other two firemen down, upholding the tradition that said the captain should always be the last man out. Handling the remaining search himself, he tried to take one last look around. Suddenly, the fire exploded, jumping up the side walls to the ceiling. Then the ceiling collapsed. John Morello found himself completely disoriented — something that happens occasionally even to veteran firemen — and he could not find his way out. He was sure at that moment that there was no escape, that he was going to die. He also became aware in some strange way that while he had been fighting the fire, it had gone from the night of January 5 to the early morning of January 6, which meant that it was Vincent's thirteenth birthday. John later remembered thinking how terrible his death would be for his son and that for the rest of Vincent's life, whenever he tried to celebrate his birthday, the birthday would be a reminder of the day his father died.

Even as that melancholy thought ran through his mind, the two firemen he had sent downstairs decided to come back to look for him; they got to the top of the stairs and called out, and he heard their voices and thereby located the stairs. He yelled at them not to move, and dove through flames, landing at the top of the stairs and then somersaulting down. It was a night he would never forget, and it made him even warier of encouraging his children in the profession. His view was that if it was a career they wanted, they would have to choose it on their own. After his son's death, though, a number of friends said to John, What do you mean you never encouraged him to be a fireman — he saw the pleasure you took from your job every day of your life, and that's what he wanted.

Vincent Morello, his mother, Pat, sometimes thought, was every bit as strong-willed as his father and every bit as determined to make his own decisions. His mechanical skills and his love of tools had been obvious from the time he was a very young child. His father had done a great many of the repairs around their house, and Vincent had faithfully followed him around, watching him carefully, wanting to help out. By

148

the time he was six or seven, when John would ask for a particular tool, needle-nose pliers or a crescent wrench, say, Vincent would know which one it was and bring it. "It was like I had created a monster," John Morello liked to say: a mechanical monster.

Being a fireman never seemed to be a possibility, in no small part because Vincent was seriously acrophobic, and firemen, of course, needed to be able to handle great heights without fear. He loved to cook and had even gone to a cooking school for a time, but after working weekends and nights in a restaurant, he decided that he preferred the hours of a mechanic to those of a chef, and he opted for the latter career. In time he went to work for the fire department as a mechanic, eventually making as much as $60,000 a year, with overtime, plus benefits and pension. He worked on Randall's Island, at the shop where all the rigs had to go four times a year for checkups. There he got to know some of the firemen, and the more he hung out with them and heard their stories, the richer their lives seemed to him.

Vincent's wife, Debi, whom he had married in 1990, thought he had become somewhat bored and restless working in the shop, where there was a lack of action and little pressure. He wanted something different. So in 1992 he took the firemen's test, did well, and was put on the waiting list. As he got closer and closer to coming aboard, Debi remembered, he became crankier and crankier, more and more restless in the shop and desperate to become a fireman. When he finally made it, in February 2000, there was the most dramatic change in his personality — she had never seen him so happy. He became a fireman when he was thirty-three, and to do so he took a pay cut of nearly fifty percent. He began by working out of Engine 283 in Brownsville, Brooklyn, then he rotated through 40/35, starting there in January of 2001.

John Morello was pleased that his son was working out of 40/35, because John had broken in there, spending four years at Ladder 35 back in the 1960s. "Dad, there's a guy here who says he worked with you when you were both *firemen*," Vincent told him. "It's got to be Terry Holden," John said, mentioning the most senior member of the house, the man who served as de facto house historian and who in 2001 was in his thirty-seventh year at the house. Vincent did very well at his father's old house. He was much admired by the other men because he had made a career switch from a privileged, cushy job to be with them, taking a huge pay cut. In addition, he was a great source of tools and other material. At the fire department it was always a problem requisitioning things through official channels; the system seemed to work as if it had been greased with molasses. But Vincent could cut through the bureaucracy in seconds, with just one phone call to one of his old colleagues. He was a valuable man and a good man: If the rest of them could do some plumbing, some electrical work, and some carpentry, Morello was a whiz at repairing cars. Suddenly the house had one of the best auto mechanics in the city, a man who seemed able to add years of life to the vehicles belonging to the men and their wives.

He was ferociously hardworking as a probie, primarily, Debi Morello thought, because he did not want to be carried by his father's reputation. He observed all probie traditions and completed all probie tasks, including stripping and washing the bedsheets every morning. Once when he came home, Debi told him that the sheets on their beds could use some washing too, but he told her he was done with bedding for the day. Because he was the junior man, he would be asked periodically to check the rigs, which meant checking the tools and the masks. But there he would be, on his back, under the truck, examining the brakes and the suspension. "Vinnie," Terry Holden would say, "I said check the rig. You don't have to do all that." And he would nod and agree and say, "Yeah, but I thought I would check this stuff as well." He was not a man who cut corners.

On the morning of September 11, John and Pat Morello were at their house on Long Island. He was taking a shower when his wife told him that a plane had hit the World Trade Center. They sat around the television set, watching the tragedy unfold, and when the first tower collapsed, John thought, *I hope to God they got all the*

151

people out — the civilians and the firemen — because that is the most complete pancake collapse I have ever seen.

He and Pat drove to Vincent and Debi's house in Queens, a home they shared with their two children, Justin, seven, and Paige, five. That afternoon he stayed on the phone, trying to get information. John called the firehouse and was mistakenly told that Ladder 35 had not responded to the call until 10:30, and that had given him considerable hope. It seemed to guarantee that his son and the men with him had not arrived until well after the worst moments of the collapse. But by 6:00 p.m. they were all worried. Debi Morello was sure that something was terribly wrong. She was sure that no matter how chaotic the situation, somehow Vincent would have managed at least one quick call. Vincent, she insisted, would have known how worried she would have been. There had been some tense moments that afternoon, with Pat Morello trying to calm her daughter-in-law by saying that Vincent might be too busy to call or perhaps there were no phones, and Debi saying, *I know my husband and he would know I was worried and he would call me.* Early Wednesday morning, John found out from the Manhattan dispatching office that Ladder 35 had gone out not at 10:30 but at 9:14, and that the entire company was missing. It was then that he heard Debi's anguished scream, the scream that seemed to be for everyone who had lost a fireman that day.

Vincent Morello was supposed to have gone off duty on the morning of September 11. However, his relief, John Daniel Marshall, who had been detailed at the last minute from nearby Engine 23, had not yet arrived. That was when Morello had offered Bob Menig a chance to wait relief, something Menig would have gladly done but for his doctor's appointment. When Marshall did arrive at the firehouse, it was just after the second plane had hit. What happened next was not entirely clear given the confusion of the moment and the eventual lack of survivors. Morello was usually with the truck, but when Marshall showed up, Morello lost his slot. But he still wanted to go — his sense of obligation was that strong. (He had just told Menig, by then driving on the Long Island Expressway to his appointment, that it was a big plane that had struck the north tower, and that he could not wait to get down there.) He apparently tried to stay on the truck as an extra man, but, some of the men at the house believe, Captain Callahan, who was in charge of the truck, would not let Morello join them on such a dangerous run. It was not a reflection on Morello. Callahan simply was unwilling to put an extra man at risk. But since labor negotiations had left the engine one man short, Morello knew there would be a vacancy there, and with the permission of Lieutenant Ginley, he jumped aboard. (Because of those last-minute decisions, the house blackboards, which listed who went out on which rig, were slightly wrong, showing Marshall going out on the engine, and Morello, misspelled "Morrello," on the truck.)

Dan Marshall, the young man who had arrived at the firehouse just as they were leaving, was a stranger to the men there. It is likely that he had been at 40/35 for all of five minutes when he went out on the last run of his life. He tossed a bag on the floor of the house, and then jumped aboard the rig; later they found the bag, which contained his personal things, including his keys and his wallet.

He had grown up in Congers, New York, one of the exurban communities about an hour north of the city. The son of a New York cop who worked in the Bronx, he was an immensely likable young man, thoughtful and balanced, and sensitive to others — "the neighborhood therapist," recalled his friend Ralph Rivera, "the person who could talk you down from your bad moods, and your worst moments of anger." When Marshall finished high school, he had done construction work before going out to Colorado. When he returned to Congers, it was with his new wife, Lori.

In the past Dan's father had pushed him to try one of the civil service jobs, and Rivera, his next-door neighbor who worked out of a firehouse in the Bronx, encouraged him to take the fire department test. Rivera, who was a little older than

Marshall, had become a fireman in 1987, and he loved the life, the sense of doing something of value; he spoke often and enthusiastically to Marshall of what being a fireman was like, and of how he thought it was the best job in the world. Lori Marshall did not agree. She thought it was far too dangerous, but Rivera was confident that it was the right job for Dan. He would be fine. What could go wrong? he had argued. What could go wrong?

Of the various job options open to Dan Marshall, becoming a firefighter looked to him far and away the best, and he had eventually taken the firemen's test and passed it. He graduated from the academy in 1999, when he was thirty-three. Rivera was not at the graduation, but he saw Marshall later that day, and the only other time he had ever seen him so happy was when his two children, John Jr. and Paige, were born. There was a huge grin on his face, from ear to ear. He had turned out to be a very good fireman, a natural, thought Dennis Fennell, who broke him in at Ladder 27 in the Bronx. Fennell thought him very hardworking and quietly ambitious — "I want to be the best," Marshall would say.

One of the things that was hard for Dan Marshall's friends to accept about his death was that he had not known the other men with him that day; that he had gone off to so horrendous a fire, surrounded by complete strangers instead of friends. Dennis Fennell wondered whether he

155

had even had time to introduce himself to all of them, and whether anyone with him had even been able to call out his first name when the collapse occurred.

SEVEN

The men went to service after service that fall. Politicians sometimes showed up and spoke, and there was a certain amount of resentment about that. Back at the firehouse afterward, the men would do a very good imitation of the politicians, using their rote phrases like: *On a day when the worst of mankind showed itself, the best of mankind answered it.* Sometimes the house was edgy now, and little things that previously would have gone unnoticed might set the men off. Part of it was the loss of Bruce Gary and Jimmy Giberson, the two men most responsible for setting and controlling the tone of the house. No one had yet taken their places.

The men were all aware of what might have been, especially those who had by chance switched their schedules with men who had died. A few days before the disaster, one of the firemen had been helping Jimmy Giberson cut a huge lock off a bicycle for a man who had lost the key and had come by the firehouse for help. Jimmy had grabbed the Partner saw and was cutting the lock off, when the saw slipped slightly and cut the other fireman's hand, putting him out of action for several days. That accident had

157

quite probably saved his life.

Sometimes they thought of what might have been had the softball team won in the play-offs the week before the attack: then Kevin Bracken, Steve Mercado, David Arce, Mike Boyle, and Jimmy Giberson would have been playing softball and might have missed the call. But who would have gone in their place? All those what-ifs and might-have-beens. . . .

Some three weeks after the events of September 11, workers going through the ruins of the south tower found the body of Bruce Gary under four stories of rubble, near the entrance to the Winter Garden atrium on West Street. From that location and other evidence, the men pieced together as best they could what they thought had happened to Bruce Gary. He had positioned the engine and was waiting there, unsure in a crisis this great what his role would be, when another fireman, without his equipment, had come by. Apparently Gary had lent the man his gear. Then Gary, the men presume, had heard a Mayday call, grabbed the engine's medical bag, and raced over to see if he could help some injured men. He was found with the medical bag alongside the bodies of several firemen and civilians.

Among the bodies found with Gary's was that of Fred Ill, the captain of Ladder 2, located on East Fifty-first Street in Manhattan. A twenty-three-year veteran, Ill was a legendary fireman, famed within the department for leading the rescue of a man who had been pushed by a disturbed homeless person off a subway platform in front of an oncoming train in April 1999. The train had stopped, but Ill was not sure if the electric current had been shut off yet. Knowing that even the slightest wrong move could be fatal, Ill had crawled beneath the train, and, with very little clearance, carried the injured man out. Afterward Ill had made sure that the man, Edgar Rivera, whose legs had been amputated, was cared for properly, that he had a decent wheelchair, and that his apartment was modified to meet his new needs. Ill even arranged for a parochial school scholarship for Rivera's son. There was some speculation in the 40/35 house that Gary might have been tending to an injured Fred Ill, when they were both killed.

The news of finding Gary's body profoundly affected the other men at the firehouse. Gary's friends believe he had been giving emergency first aid, even as the building was about to topple. But that would be Bruce Gary, doing the right thing up to the very last second of his life. A number of the men realized then that they had, in their own way, loved Gary, even though, on occasion, loving Bruce Gary was not unlike loving a human cactus.

Of the memorial services, one of the most moving was the joint November 5 service at St. Patrick's Cathedral for Mike Boyle and David Arce, the Engine 33 firefighters who had recently rotated through 40/35. (Arce was known to most of the attendees simply as Buddha, so much so that when his brother Peter eulogized David, he said to the firemen, "That's Buddha to you.") The turnout for the service was enormous, in no small part because Mike's father, Jimmy Boyle, was a warm, extroverted, immensely popular man who, as the leader of the firefighters' union, had frequently battled with Mayor David Dinkins over proposed cuts for the department. St. Patrick's was filled that day — a standing-room-only crowd. It seemed as if the entire world of New York City firefighters had come together as one immense family.

More than most men, Jimmy Boyle understood the hardship and risk inherent in this job and the pain that parents who bury their sons experience. That pain really came home to him a few weeks after his own son's memorial service, when at another ceremony he looked around and saw six senior firemen, all of them old friends of his, and all of whom had lost sons on September 11. Boyle possessed an uncannily nuanced sense of how to make other people feel comfortable in a time of grief. He always seemed to be able to get outside of his own wounds and to understand the pain of others. It did not necessarily lessen his own grief, but he knew how to hold it in in order to ease the suffering of others and to somehow take strength from the care he was bestowing. Still, for a proud and successful fireman such as Jimmy Boyle, losing a son who had followed him into the department, and who might one day have followed him as president of the Uniformed Firefighters Association, was painful beyond all imagining.

What was additionally difficult was the fact that they had found neither Mike's nor Buddha's bodies. But three months later, in early February, the workers doing the excavation at Ground Zero came upon eleven bodies of men from the Great Jones firehouse, including those, it was believed, of Boyle and Buddha, which were found within a few feet of each other. They were together at the end, as they had been for most of their lives. Four men from that house had managed to escape — the entire company had been trying to get out of the north tower just as the collapse came.

Jimmy Boyle had talked to a few of the survivors, and he discovered that his son, Arce, and the nine others had been about thirty seconds from making it out when they were buried. The sheer force of the implosion drove them five stories under. Even if they had made it out of the tower, there was no guarantee they would have lived, Jimmy Boyle discovered. Those who came out and turned north lived; those who turned either south or west died.

Mike Boyle and David Arce were to be buried next to each other in the Holy Rood Cemetery in their hometown of Westbury, Long Island — buried as if they were brothers, which was only appropriate. Jimmy Boyle took some comfort in the fact that he was certain they had finally found his son's body, and from the fact that being a firefighter had been Michael's choice and that his son had died doing exactly what he most believed in.

Marion Otten slowly began to deal with the reality of not just losing her husband but of losing so many of their friends as well. Everywhere there were reminders: the bathroom that Bruce Gary had worked on, the wallpaper that Jimmy Giberson had put up. Marion recalled a day a few years earlier when she and Michael were renovating their house because they needed more room for their three sons, Christopher, Jonathan, and Jason. They had to extend the roof to cover a new addition, and some fifteen men from the firehouse had shown up to help do it. There had not been much in the way of a formal plan for this — but somehow all of the men had arranged their shifts so they could be there. They were like some kind of Amish barn-raising crew, organizing themselves brilliantly as if they did roof extensions every day for a living. The skilled men took the specialized tasks and the others served as support troops. By noon the old roof was off, and by late afternoon a new plywood roof was on. About ten of them had shown up again when it came time to put up the Sheetrock on the new addition, Marion remembered.

Marion had always understood that the firemen were family, and whoever needed help always got help. In addition to the new roof, Michael had been planning to turn the basement into a den, and in early December, her middle son, Jonathan, had casually said something about it to Matt Malecki, one of Michael's close friends at the firehouse. Matt in turn asked Marion about the plan, and she knew immediately that these extraordinary men would one day come out in full force, transforming the basement into a handsome new den.

One of the things Marion had wrestled with in the weeks after her husband's death was what to do about a memorial service — a dilemma faced by many of the other widows as well. It was hard for her to go ahead without a body, but in the middle of October the children were still talking about the possibility of their father being alive. "How long can Daddy live?" one of them asked. "How much food and water do you need?" There had to be some kind of closure, Marion decided. She thought the service should take place before the holidays. Her old friend Reverend Scholz, the Lutheran minister who as a young pastor on Long Island had officiated at Marion and Michael's wedding, realized what a terrible dilemma it was for all of these families and how important it was for the ritual of a funeral to have the body of the deceased. But in the end, Marion held the service in mid-November, as much for her children as for anyone else.

At six and a half, Skylar Mercado, who his

163

father had hoped would grow up to be an Olympic stickball player, was at the age when little boys are most intoxicated by firehouses, and he was a special favorite of the men at 40/35. Steve Mercado had worked on the engine, but before he died, some of the truckees had been trying to recruit Skylar for the truck, though as Jimmy O'Donnell said, it was hard, because Steve had propagandized for the engine so intensely for so long. O'Donnell, a veteran truckee, had insisted to Skylar that all ladder men were great lovers, and he had even spelled it out: the *L* in lovers is for ladder, the *O* for overhaul (that is, the opening of the walls and ceiling to make sure the fire didn't spread), the *V* for vent (as in outside vent man, a truck position), the *E* for (forcible) entry, the *R* for rescue, and the *S* for search. But Skylar had seemed unmoved, and probably, O'Donnell thought, the boy had already decided long ago to be an engine man. Perhaps, O'Donnell said, they might do better one day with his younger brother, Austin.

When it first became clear to Joviana Mercado that her husband was lost, she had held back in telling Skylar the truth. But she figured that he probably already understood more than he let on, and he had probably picked up either from other kids or from the men at the firehouse that his father was dead. By the Friday after the tragedy, she felt it was time to tell Skylar the truth. When she did, he immediately wanted to know who else was missing because he had so many friends at the firehouse. She told him the names, and he knew almost all of them, save for one or two of the newest men. When she had finished, he had asked to go to the firehouse right away. He was quite nervous about it, she thought — he wondered, was it still going to be a home for him, and was he still going to be welcome there?

It had been very emotional for Skylar when he arrived at the firehouse. There were so many old friends trying to reach out to him. As he watched the men return to the house from the search parties, dirty and exhausted, he kept saying, "Where's my dad? You've got to go back and look for my dad!" With emptiness and dejection plain on their faces, the men explained that they were only taking a break, that they would go back, and that there were other search teams out there right at that moment looking for Steve.

When Joviana decided to have a service, on November 10, the men made a miniature fireman's dress uniform for Skylar, and pinned on it all his father's medals and emblems. At each memorial service the grieving families gave out small laminated cards with the deceased's name and a few details about his life, and often a prayer as well. Skylar made up his own collection of the cards for his room, and he liked to line them up and study them, as a way of remembering each man he had known.

Joviana had thought that of her two children, it would be Skylar, with greater comprehension of what had happened, who would undergo the harder time. But to her surprise it was Austin, only two and a half, who had the more difficult adjustment. Often Austin would wake up in the middle of the night and cry out for his father.

With April Ginley, grief and anger were mixed in equal parts, her friends and family thought; moreover, she wore her anger openly. Because John had been a lieutenant, and because the officers were somewhat apart from the men, she did not feel as close to the life of the firehouse as some of the other wives did. Her life had been the one she and John had shared in Warwick, and she thought of him more as a father and a husband than as a fireman.

Shortly after the attack, April toured Ground Zero, but it gave her no comfort. Some of the other widows, she knew, thought of it as sacred ground, but the tour had only served to make her angrier — not at any one person, but more at the Fates, which had robbed her of her husband overnight and had so completely changed her life. She understood that her anger seemed to make her a little different from some of the other wives, but it was the way she felt, and she could not change it; if anything, some of the therapists who were dealing with the families of the firemen believed, her anger was a more natural reaction than the stoicism exhibited by many of the other wives and families.

On the way back to the firehouse from Ground

Zero, there had been an attempt to make small talk with Bob Hickey, the fireman who had accompanied her, when April, in her own words, lost it. John, she said, had not prepared her for this, and he never thought it would happen — he never thought he was going to die on the job. Hickey had tried to comfort her, but she remained inconsolable, well outside his reach. She felt that little could have been done for most of the people in the Twin Towers that day, whereas John Ginley had been on Sixty-sixth Street along with the other men, and they could have lived. Hickey tried once more to console her, telling her that no fireman ever thinks he's going to die. "John didn't prepare you for it because none of us thinks that something like this is going to happen. None of us thinks that we're going to die," he said.

At Michael Lynch's service, April told one of his sisters, Kathleen Lynch, that she was sorry her husband had taken Michael into the building. Kathleen told her she must not think that way and recalled how many wonderful things she had heard about both John and April. But dealing with her grief remained exceptionally difficult. At Frank Callahan's memorial service, April stood in front of two older firemen and one of them had been talking about his heart attack and his bypass operation. April was irritated that the man was talking about something so *frivolous* when they were there to say good-bye to a man like Frank. She looked around and saw several older firemen with gray hair, and she thought to herself, *John will* never *have gray hair.*

She could not bear the talk about John being a hero or about how the tragedy had brought all of New York and even all of America together. Everyone kept saying how many lives had been saved because of firemen, but it brought April no comfort. Perhaps in a few months, she thought, she might see things differently. But at this point, when she put her two children to bed every night, John was not there. Throughout the fall, John's brother Bob Ginley came by often to play football with seven-year-old Connor, and she was pleased that Bob had done it, but she kept thinking that it was supposed to be John. In a year, she said, Connor was going to make his First Communion, and his father was not going to be there to see it; and someday his daughter, Taylor, was going to be married and her father was not going to be there to walk her down the aisle.

April thought her whole life was different now, different from the moment she got up in the morning to the moment she went to bed at night. She herself was a different person, she thought. All her thoughts were different. All her friends were married. She was not. April Ginley was now a single parent with two young children. She liked the old April a good deal more than the new one. That April had always known where she stood and what she wanted and needed and where her husband was. The old April was compassionate and concerned about others. The new April was much more self-absorbed and self-centered. This was not a person she liked being. She wanted her old life back. Most of all, she wanted her husband back.

Angie Callahan thought the tragedy of September 11 was much harder on a young wife such as April Ginley than it was on her. After all, she had had twenty-seven years with her man. Her and Frank's had been a strong marriage, and she had no regrets about her life, nor, she believed, would Frank have had any. She had been married to a good man, and he had done what he wanted professionally. It was a valuable life for a man: Where else, she noted, can you be brave in a time of peace, and where else can you do things that few other men do, deeds that save lives?

What had happened on September 11 was a terrible thing, but Angie knew the man she had married well enough to know that it might have been far worse had the attack happened the following day, Wednesday, September 12. On Wednesday Frank would have been off duty and his daughter Nora would have been working in the south tower. If he had lost her and his men as well, on a day when he was not working, it would have been intolerable for him, leaving him with a life that was no longer acceptable. Angie could barely imagine what it would have been like to live with Frank under those circumstances.

169

As she prepared for her husband's December 10 service, Angie had to deal with the absence of his body. It was not that hard for her, although she knew this issue was difficult for some of the other families. It depended, she thought, on one's view of spirituality. Everyone has his or her own beliefs. She believed that once the soul left the body, it was over. The body's mission was done. She had accepted her husband's life as it was, and now she accepted his death.

His memorial service was supposed to be the last of all for the men from 40/35. That was only fitting, as Captain Jim Gormley said in his eulogy for Callahan: Captains were the first in and, by both oath and tradition, the last out. Callahan was a fellow captain and, Gormley said, more than a friend or a brother. He was a comrade, and unlike friends and brothers, comrades held one another to higher standards. They could not forgive one another's mistakes because the price of those mistakes was so terrible. "When a comrade dies, we miss them," he said. "We regret words unspoken, we remember the love, we grieve the future without them. We are also proud. Proud to have known a good man, a better man than ourselves. We respect the need for him to leave, to rest."

The service was held at Alice Tully Hall in Lincoln Center, a place the firehouse had always protected, but which the Callahans as a couple had rarely visited. Angela Callahan loved Mozart, and that past August, just a few weeks before the terrible day, she had gotten tickets to a Mostly Mozart program at Lincoln Center. She had asked her husband to go with her, and he agreed, albeit somewhat reluctantly — it was not really his kind of thing. They parked a block from the firehouse, and afterward, on their way home, they saw the men in front of it, and they waved. She suggested they go in and have a cup of coffee, but he did not want to — perhaps they would have teased him about going to hear Mozart. But that was Frank, Angela thought.

After September 11, Angela visited Ground Zero with some of the men, and she was staggered by the destruction. It was beyond her comprehension. Kurt Vonnegut's *Slaughterhouse Five* was one of her favorite books, and so she had read descriptions of the worst tragedies of World War II, but this just overwhelmed her. It was like visiting a different city in a different country.

Angela Callahan worried often about the men who had survived. She was fearful that some of them were being stretched too thin, devastated by the fact that they had survived when so many of their friends had not, pulled by a sense of responsibility to the families of those who had died, and yet still committed to their own families. In the early weeks and months after the attack, there was so much going on demanding immediate attention that everyone seemed to be doing all right. But Angela worried about the coming dark, gray winter months, when there would be more time to think about things.

Angie Callahan was all too aware that the macho culture of the firehouse was such that men were not supposed to go for therapy, that by the codes of the firehouse, they were to tough out their troubles and that therapy would be seen as a sign of weakness. Some of the men did go for therapy, though, even if somewhat uneasily. (Reverend Scholz helped find counseling for many of them.) Once while eating lunch around the firehouse kitchen table, Ray Pfeifer told Mike Kotula that no, he was not going to see a therapist, but Kotula said that he *was* seeing a therapist, and that he quite liked her; the way he thought of it was that he was visiting Mr. Rogers, but a Mr. Rogers *with breasts.*

Kevin Shea was not exactly sure where he fit in now, and he wondered whether there was some undertow of resentment from the others because he alone of the 40/35 men who went out that day had managed to survive. There was no doubt that he had been badly injured that day and that he was lucky to be alive. His entire body had been black and blue. He had suffered a serious concussion and a broken neck — with fractures of the C-5, C-6, and C-7 vertebrae. The doctors, he was told, took the tibia of a cadaver, ground it down to the right size, and replaced his fifth cervical vertabra with it. Ninety percent of the tissue of one testicle had to be removed, along with ten percent of the other one. For several weeks he was relatively immobile, and he had to wear a neck brace into mid-December.

When he returned to the house, he felt somewhat uncomfortable. He wondered whether when the other men looked at him, they saw something wrong, as if he were wearing some kind of scarlet letter. Somehow he felt less connected than he had expected. Perhaps, he thought, it was all in his mind, that he was taking his own guilt and transferring it onto their view of him. But something was wrong. One day he was talking to another fireman and the man broke off the conversation quickly and told him, "I'm sick of your shit. Just go away." When he had tried to talk to one of his friends, asking if he had done anything wrong, his friend had answered, "Kevin, this is just not the right time to talk about it."

At the memorial service for Frank Callahan, Captain Gormley spoke of the men who had died that day and then made a brief reference to Kevin Shea: "Kevin, we are joyful to have you back." That had been reassuring, his first official welcome back into the fold. He was not sure, however, what his future as a fireman was. He wanted eventually to go back to full-time duty, but the decisions on that were to be made by the department, not by himself.

Some of the firemen thought that no small part of Shea's problem was his perpetual innocence, a quality that made him seem out of sync with the current mood of the house. They were bothered that he wore his doubts about what had happened to him far too openly. In December Shea started talking to a bright young writer named David Grann, on assignment from *The New York Times Magazine*, about what had happened on September 11 and how he was wrestling with his doubts about how he had behaved. Grann's article quite accurately reflected Shea's anguish — although not the broader view of Shea's superiors, who thought the young fireman's painful self-doubt was the most natural response from a survivor of a catastrophe, especially the sole survivor of a firehouse shift. But what was quite stunning about the article, when it was published on Sunday, January 13, 2002, were the headlines written by the editor of the magazine, Adam Moss, headlines that were apparently jazzed up despite objections from Grann. The magazine's cover trumpeted: "Amnesia at Ground Zero: Was the Firefighter a Hero or a Coward?" Inside the magazine, running above the article, were the words, "Which Way Did He Run?" followed by: "After Firefighter Kevin Shea lost his memory on Sept. 11, he set out to discover if he was a hero or, as he alone feared, a coward when the towers collapsed."

When the article was published, it created a furor at the firehouse. The idea that some editor, who had been nowhere near the danger on that apocalyptic day, might cast doubt over the actions of a man so wounded and now so vulnerable seemed to the men almost inconceivable. If anything, the incident seemed to underline a cultural conflict in the city itself — between those who always sought to emphasize what was new and exciting and those who abided by more traditional codes, in which there was great sensitivity about adding more pain to existing pain. (After Shea's fiancée, Stacy Hope Herman, called Moss to protest the headlines, he eventually called her back and apologized about the use of the word *coward,* saying he had not understood that the word, one that was not used in the world of firemen, would be seen as so explosive.)

There is a quick flash of videotape that shows Lieutenant John Ginley, Michael Lynch, Steve Mercado, and Mike D'Auria as they descend the stairs into the lobby of Building Four and head for the lobby of the south tower. The tape runs in slow motion for about ten seconds, and though no one is sure of the exact time it was shot, it obviously takes place well into the disaster — the air is full of debris. Some authorities believe it was filmed a little before 10:00 a.m., just prior to the two terrible collapses. It is easy to identify the men. They are loaded up with gear, and their expressions are unusually stoic. Their brothers from 40/35 find it almost unbearable to watch the brief clip, because they can imagine what the men already know about their chances of surviving, and yet they are going forward, with no panic or fear on their faces. They are, in the fire-fighting lexicon, calm, and they are doing the right thing. It is a haunting moment, and the videotape reveals with rare intimacy what brave men look like at the worst moment that the Fates can present.

When Stephanie Luccioni, Michael Lynch's fiancée, viewed the tape, she found it jarring at first — this last glimpse of him alive, so strong and unbending at such a terrible moment. But then she decided that the tape was his way of saying good-bye to her, of saying, *This is my duty, and I am going to do it.* This made her even prouder of him, and she felt blessed by the fact that she had loved and been loved by a man of such honor.

Stephanie was determined to go on with her life, but occasionally when she wanted to feel that Michael was still around, she played that last tape of him and the other men descending into the hell of the burning World Trade Center.

Some five months after the tragedy, Ray Pfeifer heard from John Lynch, Michael Lynch's father, about footage shot by a contract cameraman working for one of the networks that almost surely showed the men of Ladder 35 as they entered one of the towers. Pfeifer spent some time tracking down the tape — which happened to be from the same photographer who caught the engine as they headed toward the south tower — and when he got it, he brought it to the firehouse. It was both fascinating and haunting to watch the video — the clarity with which it showed the collapse of the south tower was almost unbearable to see. One minute the giant structure is still standing, proud but badly damaged, smoke pouring out of its upper stories, and then, with an unbelievable force driving it, the collapse began, windows popping out, floor by floor, ever so sequentially, like a series of dominoes toppling. And then there was nothing but smoke and dust.

What made the video even more dramatic, indeed almost unendurable for the men in the firehouse, was the brief section that showed the men of Ladder 35 as they made their fateful entry into the south tower. One morning in early February of 2002, the men of 40/35 played the video over and over at the firehouse, trying to identify everyone on the tape. Because of the video's erratic quality, caused by having been shot under such hectic, frightening circumstances, it was impossible to get a sense of exactly when it was shot, but the men at the firehouse believed it showed their brothers entering the south tower about ten minutes before the collapse.

There they were, men who had once been the closest of friends, men who had once dominated this very room with the force of their personalities, in the final moments of their lives. It was hard to identify the individuals because, in addition to the erraticism, the video had been shot at some distance. Nonetheless, there they were, moving quickly in single file toward an entrance. "Okay — now watch, that's the captain," said Ray Pfeifer. Then right behind him, staying very close, was the most junior among the firemen, Dan Marshall — and that was according to tradition: the most junior man, staying right next to the officer. "There! That's Mikey Otten and that's Michael Roberts, and that's Kevin Bracken," said Pfeifer. And everyone agreed with him.

The only figure about whom there was some doubt was that of a man who entered the building a few seconds ahead of Callahan. The debate was whether it was Jimmy Giberson. The men questioned why Giberson would have gone in ahead of the captain. "He holds his tools exactly the way Jimmy did, the exact same angle," said Pfeifer, and Anthony Rucco and Joe Mackey, who were watching, agreed. So did Terry Holden, who thought he could pick out Giberson's immense mustache. But they were puzzled why Giberson would be out in front.

Then Mike Kotula arrived, and they ran the tape several times for him. Kotula had been exceptionally close to Giberson and had taken his death very hard. Now, as he watched, he was absolutely sure it was Jimmy. "That's him! No doubt about it!" said Kotula. "Then, why is he out in front?" one of the others asked. "Jimmy was always in front. Always. With those long legs, you couldn't keep up with him. And no one was going to stop him on something like this," Kotula said.

One of the men asked Kotula if he was *absolutely* sure it was Giberson. Yes, said Kotula. "Look at the way he holds his tools. That's Jimmy. Look at how long his legs are. See, his coat seems to be short on his body because he's so tall. That's Jimmy. No one else."

The men sat there, playing the tape again and again, getting one last look at their friends, walking into the building from which they would not come out alive.

John Morello spoke at his son's memorial service, and he spoke beautifully. He was a man who used words exceptionally well. He asked the people in the church for their forbearance, because he was not well prepared for the occasion — it was usually sons who were called on to eulogize their fathers. But then he described Vincent as a son and a husband and father, and the richness of life ahead of him, and how well he had wanted to do everything. For the first few days after the attack, when John was in the shower, he would reach out to touch the tiles, tiles that Vincent had installed — touching them, he thought, was like reaching out and touching his son. And then, he told the mourners, he would weep.

Debi Morello was left with two young children, Justin, seven, and Paige, five. Debi had worked at HBO as an executive assistant, and she knew she would work again, but her main job now, she believed, was to be there for her children. Even so, she was planning to become a teacher and was going to arrange her schedule at home so she could take courses at Queens College; she hoped to get her degree and start teaching at precisely the moment when her children did not need her full-time at home anymore.

Her main job now, though, was to keep life as normal as possible for Justin and Paige. The loss was searing, the destruction of her family as it had once been, a family torn right down the center. But she was resolved not to feel sorry for herself. The transition to a new life was overwhelming, but she did not feel, with the daily needs of her children, that she could afford to think too much of the past.

Something that bothered Debi was the effect of the outpouring of sympathy on her children. One of the dangers, she thought, was all the attention they were getting, which included too many presents from strangers; she was uneasy with the idea that the children might think that they were somehow being rewarded because of the death of their father. Over-rewarded, even. She understood the impulse behind it, that there were millions of people who felt that the attack had been aimed at them as much as it had been at those who had suffered the immediacy of the pain, and that this was their way of trying to say that. But generous as the gestures were, she was afraid they would confuse her children. There was other potential psychological damage as well. In the minds of her children, becoming a hero now meant that you had to die, and they wanted no part of that. Justin now told her that he was not going to be a fireman when he grew up for just that reason.

One thing that made things even more difficult was that Vincent had not been permanently stationed at the firehouse, and so she did not know very many of the wives there. The previous summer, at a picnic in the Bronx organized by Steve Mercado, she had gotten to know and like two of the wives, Marion Otten and Jennifer Liang, and she stayed in touch with them after the tragedy. She often pondered what had gone on in Vincent's mind in those final moments. One of the firemen she knew told her that if Vinnie had known the building was going to collapse, he would not have gone in. But there was never going to be any answer to that, she thought.

Vincent's older brother, Marc, also a firefighter, returned to his firehouse in Brooklyn, Ladder 147, which was difficult for him in the weeks right after the tragedy because that house had not lost anyone. Though Marc loved his colleagues, somehow it was for the moment a little hard to be there. But then he heard that Ladder 35, devastated as it was, needed men for temporary duty, and he volunteered to work there for a few months. "Are you doing this for your brother?" his father asked him, and Marc thought about it, and said yes, he was. But it was the right thing to do, at least temporarily, be-

181

cause his own terrible sense of loss seemed to parallel that of so many of the men at 40/35. It was good for him to be there, he said, and perhaps it was good for them that the brother of one of the men who had been lost wanted to be there with them.

Vincent Morello would have been thirty-five years old on January 6, 2002. One of the things he and his pals loved to do — and they had to be careful how often they did it, because none of them made that much money — was to celebrate at a good steak house. On the occasion of his birthday this year, Marc Morello took a table for fourteen at Bryant & Cooper, a steak house in Roslyn, Long Island. He invited all of Vincent's buddies, and set a place for Vincent. Beside it he put a shot of Ketel One vodka mixed with 7Up, which was Vincent's favorite drink. They ordered a birthday cake and sang happy birthday to him, all of them weeping. Thus did they celebrate the short but rich life of Vincent Scott Morello.

The death of his son, Richard Otten thought, was by far the hardest thing he and his wife, Terry, had ever undergone. Three or four days after the tragedy he went down to Ground Zero and walked the scene as best he could. He asked the various men in charge a great many questions, and then he simply stood and stared at the wreckage. As a former fire captain, he tried to visualize what had happened that morning in the terrible confusion and chaos, what the men in command had been forced to do at a moment when all their codes and their traditions suddenly collided with a reality that was far too painful. Richard needed to understand it, or at least to understand it as best as anyone would be able to understand it. He looked out at the site for a very long time, surveying the enormity of the collapse. It was like nothing he had ever seen. Whatever frail hope for his son's survival that he might have been holding on to, drained out of him as he looked out over the rubble.

Richard Otten tried as best he could to accept it, to accept the fact that all of this was in some ways beyond him. A local television reporter had come by and had told him that a number of the fathers of firemen whom he had interviewed had seemed to accept their loss more stoically than other people might have. Probably Richard Otten decided, that was true, though in no way did it lessen the pain. He had been a fireman, and he had always known the risks, and his son had known those risks too. Michael had loved the life, and he had made his own choices — he had died doing his duty. So Richard Otten had to accept that — it was one way of understanding.

Small gestures helped too. In Deer Park, New York, the town board voted to honor Michael's memory by changing the name of the street that his parents lived on from Headline Road to Michael Otten Memorial Road.

Jimmy and Susan Giberson had been separated at the time of his death, but she was pleased that the separation was amicable and that they had remained close. She was proud too of how good and loving a father he had been with their three daughters, Erika, Kari, and Sara. All three girls were talented swimmers, and the fact that Jimmy had spent what would be the final Saturday of his life with the girls at the Great Kills Swim Club in Staten Island pleased her immensely. She was grateful as well that he had spent his entire career at one firehouse, because that meant that she was close to and had the support of many of the men there, such as Mike Kotula, and many of the wives as well, including Marion Otten, whom she found to be a wonderful, strong person. The Ottens and the Gibersons had been particularly close because, though the Ottens had three boys and the Gibersons three girls, their children were roughly the same age, and that had helped to forge a considerable bond. In February, Susan Giberson joined Marion Otten and the other widows when they held a reunion at a restaurant near the firehouse. She felt very much at home.

On December 7 the Lynch family held a memorial service celebrating the life of Michael Lynch at St. Frances de Chantal in Throgs Neck, Bronx. It was the church Michael had attended as a boy. Coming as it did soon after the

Thanksgiving holiday, the family included in the program a letter Michael had written at Thanksgiving when he was nine years old, thanking his parents for all the things they had done for him that year, and assuring them that "when Thanksgiving dinner is over, I will be 2 pounds heavier."

It was hard to do the service without a body — like a dress rehearsal for a funeral, Jack Lynch thought — that was why they made it a celebration of Michael's life, with his brothers, sister, and close friends speaking of his love of life. Without the service, Jack and Kathleen Lynch felt, there might have been no closure. The service was very emotional because of its size; the Lynch family had an enormous number of friends, and they all seemed to have shown up. In addition, the firemen from both Ladder 32 in the Bronx, to which Michael was normally attached, and from Engine 40, to which he had been attached the day of the tragedy attended in full force. There was a huge overflow crowd, much of which was seated downstairs, to listen to the service piped in over loudspeakers.

When the service was over, it was in fact not over for Jack Lynch. He continued to go to Ground Zero, visiting there almost every other day. He was hoping that the workers would eventually find the bodies of his son and of his son's colleagues. It was, he said, the most elemental impulse of a parent, to look out for and protect his child, and this was his last offering for his son. He was quite sure they would one day find the bodies of his son, Lieutenant Ginley, Steve Mercado, and Mike D'Auria — the four men caught in the brief video clip of the engine. The clip also showed Glen Pettit, a police cameraman going in with them, and in mid-December Pettit's body was uncovered near the south wall of the south tower. This gave Jack Lynch renewed hope. He was convinced that as the excavation continued, the bodies of the men from Engine 40 would someday be discovered. It seemed to him to be a father's responsibility to watch over the site, and so he kept going there. By February, he was quite sure he knew where the remaining bodies were, buried under what had become a makeshift road used by workers to cart away the wreckage. It would be at least another month, he knew, before workers would be able to excavate beneath this road.

Jack Lynch spent so much time at Ground Zero that he became a member of a new, informal community there — a community of men like himself who had lost a child and who had come to watch over the workers and to keep their own vigil. They had, not surprisingly, a special, albeit terrible, bond to each other, and there was rarely much need for words. When they would meet for the first time, often through introductions that were made quite tentatively, the fathers would simply give the names of their sons and daughters and what they had been doing that day at the towers — fireman, Cantor Fitzgerald,

Windows on the World. As they offered their terse descriptions, there would almost always be a few tears shed.

In the meantime, Jack Lynch understood that there was a void in his and his wife's lives, and in the lives of all their children, and that nothing else would ever be quite the same, that a part of them was missing. There would *always* be a part of them all that was missing. The tragedy, he said, was the only thing in all his life that had truly challenged his faith.

At 3:00 a.m. on January 1, 2002, workers found the body of Michael D'Auria. For his mother, Nancy Marra, the news was at once upsetting and a vast relief. It meant that they would have to go through another service, but it also meant that there would be a genuine finality to it. The body had apparently been found relatively intact. Marra had watched television constantly in the months after September 11, and when she saw video clips of Ground Zero, all she had been able to think was, *Michael's down there somewhere.* She knew that it was not really the body that was so important after death, but the spirit, and at the first service, they had celebrated the wonder of his spirit. But nonetheless, without the body, she felt she had been unable to say a proper good-bye to her son. After all, his body had come from her body, and it was a body that she had hugged countless times. The body mattered.

After they found him, Marra and her daughter Christina D'Auria Rinaldi drove down to the New York University Hospital morgue and waited for the body to be brought there in a hearse. Then they drove back to the funeral home behind the hearse, and at the funeral home, Marra was allowed to spend some time alone with the body, and that was a great source of solace. The funeral service, held Saturday, January 5, 2002, in Staten Island, almost four months after his death, was emotional for her, and for Michael's father, Carmen D'Auria, who had come up from Florida for it.

Carmen D'Auria had been apart from Nancy for many years, and because his son had lived with Nancy, Carmen felt that he had been removed from his son's life more than he had wanted to be. At the first service, he had been sensitive to his treatment by the firemen, priests, and other members of the family. Those tensions had been increased because he suffered from multiple sclerosis, and did not get around very well. At the second service the men from 40/35 made an extra effort to make the day as bearable as possible for him. He showed up at the firehouse early that morning, long before the service, and he asked to ride out to Staten Island on the engine in his son's seat. The firemen were glad to accommodate him, understanding that this was his last attempt to reach out and touch his son's life.

★ ★ ★

On March 21, 2002, rescue workers, digging through the rubble at almost precisely the point where Jack Lynch thought the bodies would be found, did indeed discover eleven bodies, including those of Lieutenant John Ginley, Vince Morello, and Michael Lynch, all three of whom had set out with Engine 40. The men doing the extrication came on the first body in the early afternoon and were able to identify Michael Lynch because of the markings inside his gear, and then within minutes found the bodies of Ginley and Morello. The extrication was a slow, difficult process, and as the workers labored through the afternoon the word went out and members of all three immediate families began to arrive. There were several men from 40/35 there and others joined them — some of them fighting back tears. The regular workers stepped aside and allowed the members of the firehouse to dig out the body of Vincent Morello, the last of the three to be freed from the rubble. Then the medical examiner came and checked the remains, which were put in body bags, and then the body bags were draped with flags. At about 9:30 p.m., a slow, mournful procession took place as the bodies were carried by comrades to waiting ambulances.

That meant that the only body still to be found from the engine was that of Steve Mercado. The three families, the Ginleys, Lynches, and Morellos, like the Boyle family, now had to await

189

DNA confirmation. The emotions triggered were infinitely complex; some degree of relief that the bodies had finally been found and that a process of extremely painful waiting was over, and yet no small amount of pain and grief that wounds which had not yet healed would be so raw and open once again. For the Mercado family and the families of those who rode on Ladder 35, the small, daily rituals of life became, if anything, even harder, and it made their status — still waiting, suspended as they were without hope and without bodies, and trying to accept the idea of death without a body — that much more difficult.

AUTHOR'S NOTE

I live on Sixty-seventh Street on the West Side of Manhattan, some three and a half blocks from the Engine 40, Ladder 35 firehouse. My family and I have lived in our apartment for twenty-one years, but before the tragedy of September 11, I had never been inside the firehouse. I had passed it many times, and I had often seen the men at work in our neighborhood, and, however distantly, I had admired them — in New York there is always on the part of average citizens a quiet sense of admiration for firemen, for their courage, for the highly professional and immensely good-natured way they go about their jobs, and for the fact that they constantly have to deal with terrifying fires in the high-rises that surround us. In this book, Captain Jim Gormley recalls the Lionel Hampton Fire, one that occurred five blocks from my home in January 1997. I distinctly remember the great number of fire trucks assembled that day, although I, like most civilians, did not have any sense at the time of how frightening the fire was to the men who had to confront it and put it out.

September 11, of course, changed everything. My most lasting image of that morning will always be of the firefighters going into the Twin Towers just as everyone else was trying to leave them. Going back to my days as a young reporter covering first the Civil Rights movement and then the Vietnam War, I have always admired acts of uncommon courage on the part of ordinary people. The courage displayed by the firemen on September 11, though, was really beyond my comprehension. Even with elite combat units, when a soldier runs across a field of fire to carry off a wounded buddy, he is doing it for a pal; with firehouses, it is important to remember, the firefighters, in keeping with their professional code, perform acts of exceptional courage to save complete strangers. That fact alone remains incredibly sobering for those of us who live essentially risk-free lives.

When Graydon Carter, the editor of *Vanity Fair*, asked me to go over to the 40/35 firehouse and learn and write about the men, I was eager to take on the assignment. His instinct for a story, the latitude he gives a writer to pursue it, and his innate trust in his writers, are some of the things that make him special as an editor. I want to thank him and also Doug Stumpf, my editor at the magazine and on this book. Doug and I have worked together closely for fourteen years now, at three separate institutions, and he has always had an extraordinary sense of — and faith in — the kind of work I am capable of doing.

I first visited the firehouse in mid-October and spent most of the next two and a half months there. One of the things that makes a career in journalism both pleasurable and valuable over time — for me, a very long time — is the reward that comes in discovering, again and again, the nobility of ordinary people. Rarely have I had so strong a sense of that as when I was with the firemen. More, there are very few stories that I have written in my fifty years as journalist that have been so personally rewarding. Though I was an outsider who knew no one at the firehouse and was dealing with a great many people at a time when they were in considerable pain, I was treated with remarkable grace, generosity of spirit, and, finally, good humor by everyone there. From the start, the families of the men from 40/35 who died on September 11 granted me the most important thing they had: their trust.

One of the things that is very attractive about the firehouse from the perspective of a reporter is that it is the rare spin-free zone. In an America where the job of inflating the reputations of people with negligible larger social value has become a major growth industry, firemen do what they do because they love doing it, not because they want the plaudits of outsiders. Instead, what they want most is the respect of their peers. In some ways, theirs is a hermetically sealed world: Very few of their heroics are ever written about, and most of the great stories within the world of fire fighting are passed on as part of an oral tradition, rather than in the city's daily newspapers or on local television newscasts.

Because of their traditions and because of the way firefighters live and how intimate their knowledge is of one another, you cannot con anyone in a firehouse. Within the house, you're always being measured; it is a mandatory process given the constancy of the danger the men face. The contrast between their world and some of the other, more ego-driven and materialistic worlds that I have covered in recent years is striking. Even as I was going over to the firehouse every day, the Enron scandal was breaking, serving as a daily reminder of the exact opposite kind of leadership and values.

Let me then express my thanks to all of the people who helped in making this book possible, and especially to the widows — Angie Callahan, April Ginley, Marion Otten, Joviana Perez-Mercado, Jennifer Liang, Susan Giberson, and Debi Morello — and to Teresa Ivey and Stephanie Luccioni, who shared so much with me. They have my gratitude for their kindness and openness. I want to also thank the parents and kin of the firemen for their help, in particular the members of the Roberts, Lynch, Morello, and D'Auria families.

To the men of 40/35 I owe a special debt for their candor and their trust. They accepted me on faith and I cherish their honesty and the pleasure of their company, starting with Captain James Gormley, who welcomed me into the firehouse and set the tone for the courtesies I received. In addition, firefighter Sean Newman, formerly a reporter for Reuters, was uncommonly helpful in serving as an unofficial ambassador between the world of the firehouse and the world of journalism and in helping to minimize misconceptions and mistakes. Also, the Reverend Robert Scholz, the pastor of a neighborhood Lutheran church who has helped find counseling for many of the men in the months since the terrorist attack, generously vouched for me early in the game.

I want to also thank Stephen Levey for giving me so much help on both the magazine article and the book. At *Vanity Fair*, Punch Hutton and Matt Trainor were exceptionally helpful. In addition, I want to thank Carolyn Parqueth for typing my notes so quickly, Lisa Queen for watching out for me, and Santa Varma and Jeff Seroy for their assistance. At Hyperion, thanks go to Will Schwalbe, Bob Miller, Ellen Archer, Kiera Hepford, and Stella Connell. And thanks as well to my usual support team: Marty Garbus, Bob Solomon, Philip Roome, Linda Drogin, Ken Starr, John Phelan, and Dr. Stephen Marks.